Foreword   By Rear Admiral Sir Robert Wo...

It is an honour and a priviledge to have been inv...
cial book. The production of a new edition of Pe...
work is a wonderful way to celebrate Peggy's 100th birthday! Congratulations to
Peggy and her family!

The Story of Port Navas is a treasure to possess, not only for those of us lucky
enough to live here, but for everyone who has any interest in the history of Cornwall, from all aspects... social, geological and industrial. This enlarged and updated
version of the original book has been painstakingly researched by Peggy's son, John,
who, as a surgeon, has an eye for colourful history which tracks the activities of
this special Cornish haven throughout the years. Neolithic adventures, Bronze Age
happenings, Mining, shipping of Granite for Nationally renowned Monuments, such
as Nelson's Column! ..[one block of which still remains on the Lower Quay..!], and
some great adventures supporting Special Operations in WW11....The Oystery still
remains as a working unit. Mines and Quarries do not..

The history of the families that have lived in the vicinity throughout the centuries is
well documented and those who live here today are mentioned..

On a personal note, my flying career within the Royal Navy brought me to this area
in 1958 and I moved, with my family, to Trenarth in 1967.. [the year I took ownership of Mooring no:31, now 1/2 a century ago!]. Later we lived at Drift Farm, during
which time I became Flag Officer Royal Yachts, in command of H.M.Y. Britannia..
I brought her up the River as close to Port Navas as possible, turning off Dur-gan!!
We moved to Rose Hill in 2006, with Mooring no:31 at the bottom of the gar-den!!

Thank you, Peggy, for this inspirational story. I thoroughly commend this
fascinating book to all those with a love for this Place and to anyone with an
interest in Cornish
history....They will not be able to put it down!

The Creek at High Tide from the Upper Quay, November 2015. A house on the far bank was destroyed by a German bomb in 1942 (Page 84. Photo courtesy of Kate West, on her i phone 5(s))

This book is for all who have a general interest in matters Cornish, or a particular interest in 19th century industrial developments of granite, mining, oysters and coastal shipping., and of course direct or indirect connection with the neighbourhood, The entire text has been revised, with four new chapters, two new appendices. The number of illustrations is tripled. The account is as accurate as possible, although errors are inevitable. Selected maps are placed at the back for ease of access. An index has been added. Allowance is needed for the quality of old images! It is hoped this new edition will serve as a useful reference.

Any profits will be donated to local Charities, benefiting from Gift Aid.

Acknowledgements

This has been most emphatically a community effort, involving many members of the village. By their generous contributions, comments, editing, help, and proof reading, this new edition became possible. Below are friends to whom I owe particular thanks.

Pat Cross, Michael Danby, Dougie Down, Nicky Finan, Dilys Gardiner, Don Garman, Margaret Green, David Kerslake, Shirley Knowles, Jeff Meadows, Lucie Nottingham, Ron Prior, Brian Spargo, Ronnie Rashleigh, Peter and Margaret Scott, Fran Stuart, Sally Thomas, Sue Thomas, Richard Tiptaft, Dee Watt, Philip Webber, Kate West, Roger and Bernice Wickens, Betty Williams, Rear Admiral Sir Robert Woodard.

Other major sources of new material were obtained through the kindness of the County Records Office (CRO), Royal Institute for Cornwall, National Maritime Museum Falmouth (NMM), Constantine Museum (CM), National Newspaper Archives, Find My Past, and "Constantine in Cornwall" by Charles Henderson, (HCIC)1932, (now available on line), Helford Estuary Historic Audit (2000), South West Granite by Peter Stanier. References and sub notes are provided at the end of each chapter.

Contents

Chapter 1   Introduction

Chapter 2   **The Geological Setting of Port Navas** by Professor Peter Scott
An account of the geological background and features of the area

Chapter 3   **Prehistory**
Local humans in Mesolithic, Neolithic, Bronze age, Iron age, Roman and post Roman to Medieval times

Chapter 4   **Medieval Manors and Farms**
Overview of the principal estates of the neighbourhood

Chapter 5   **The Mayns of Ponsaverran**
Summarising the dynasty which created the modern village

Chapter6   **A Fledgling Port Navas and the Granite trade**
Early Port Navas as a port , commercial structure, and community

Chapter 7   **Mining**
Summarising the principal mines of the neighbourhood

Chapter 8   **Fishing and Oyster Farming**
Details of the oyster fishery from medieval through to the present.

Chapter 9   **Granite, Iron Ore, Coal, Timber, Guano, Grain and Lime**
Life in the evolving 19th and early 20th century Village up to WW 2

Chapter 10   **Church and Chapel**
Religion cemented the community in the 19th and early 20th century

Chapter 11   **Mariners of the Busy Little Port**
An account of the seamen, and their ships which were the bedrock of the community's commercial days

Chapter 12   **1945 to 2015**
People and events of the last 70 years

Appendix A   **Some Vessels of the Port**

Appendix B   **Skills of the Granite trade**

Appendix C   **Maps**

Index

List of Illustrations and acknowledgements

Cover: Autumn Creek Head, (Geoff Meadows).
Page 4 : High tide from the club, Kate West.

1. First visit 1930.(Nicky Finan)
2. Geological map (Nicky Finan)
3. Mylor bed slates. (Peter Scott0
4. Carmenellis granite. (Peter Scott)
5. Flora 10,000 years ago. (Shepperd)
6. Creekhead, 300 B.C.
7. Calamansack Round. (Google Earth).
8. Life in the round . (Fran Stuart)
9. Round House (Fran Stuart)
10. Round House Village
11. Trenarth front (Lucie Nottingham)
12. Mrs Trerice 1930's (Lucie Nottingham)
13. Trenarth yard, by Tom Cross
14. Jonathan Mayn's Advert 1830
15. Lower Calamansac House (Mrs Collins)
16. Cellar scribings, Lower Calamansack
17. Lower Calamansack quay (Shepperd)
18. Bosahan Quarry (Constantine Museum).
19. Maen Tol pre 1869
20. "Lady of Avenel " (NMMC Falmouth).
21. "Fanny Crossfoeld" (Sally Thomas)
22. "Fanny Crossfield"
23. Anna Maria Mine maps (CRO)
24. Mine workers. (Constantine Museum)
25. Anna Maria Plan . (Constanine Museum)
26. Stealing oysters
27. Royal Visit 1921 (Constantine Museum)
28. Royal Visit 1938 (Constantine Museum)
29. Oyster Farm 1934 (Brian Spargo)
30. Oyster Farm 1945   (Brian Spargo)
31. Working the Dredge (Brian Spargo)
32. " Duchy"   (Brian Spargo)
33. Days Harvest up the Beach (Brian Spargo)
34. Loading oysters for London (Brian Spargo)
35. Village Map 1878   (Cornwall CRO)
36. Trenarth Cottage
37. Village centre 1905 (Brian Spargo)
38. Village centre 1910(Constantine Museum).
39. Creek head 1910 (Brian Spargo)
40. Creek head 1920 (Constantine Museum).
41. Ponsavarren Estate Map

42. Washing Pool (Constantine Museum).
43. "Queen of the Fal" 1930's (NMMC)
44. Quay road 1926   (Brian Spargo
45. Scotch derrick 1875 (NMMC)
46. Swivel base 2015   (Shepperd
47. Creek head 1910   (C Museum)
48. Upper Quay 1920   (Brian Spargo)
49. Seine nets 1920   (Brian Spargo)
50. Creek 1930 (Constantine Museum)
51. Upper quay, late 1930's (Brian Spargo)
52. Alfred Hawkes car (Brian Spargo)
53. Pennance 1930
54. Croft 1925   (Dilys Gardiner)
55. Bate's shop 1920 (Constantine museum)
56. Bate's shop 1922 (Constantine museum)
57. Captain Steven Bate 1940   (CM)
58. Captain Tom Collings and Daughter
59. Penjerrick Bus, 1930's (Constantine M)
60. Village group Ponsavarren
61. Rendles c 1930 (Constantine Museum)
62. Sub Lieutenant Howard Rendle (CM)
63. HMS Sunbeam
64. Trebah 1944 (CRO)
65. Upper Quay early 1930's (Brian Spargo)
66. Upper Quay 1930 (Brian Spargo)
67. Lower Quay, 1930 (Brian Spargo)
68. Creek head 1930 (Constantine museum)
69. New Chapel 1920 (Constantine museum)
70. New Chapel 1990
71. Chapel 2015 (Shepperd)
72. "Water Lily"
73. John Doyle gravestone
74. Upper Quay about 1950 (C Museum)
75. Mayn Cottage
76. Garage with Pumps (C Museum)
77. Brian Spargo (Constantine Museum)
78. Walter Warren (Constantine Museum)
79. Creek head 1961
80. Creek head mid 1960's
81. Constantine band
82. "Birowlie"
83. Creek 1960's
84. Village residents 2010(Dilys Gardiner)
85. Penpoll Mill

86. Knibb's Engineering Works
87. Knibb's Engineering Works
88. Memorial to Frances Knibb
89. Neolithic Hide ship (Ron Prior)
90. Bronze age merchant
91. Romano Gallic Merchant (Fran Stuart)
92. Medieval Knarr
93. Lateen rigged 14th century merchant (S.Knowles)
94. Tudor Merchant
95. "Lady of Avenel" (Poole Museum)
96. Figurehead (Poole Museum)
97. "Guiding Star"
98. "Guiding Star"
99. "Howard"
100. "Flying Foam" wreck and site
101. "Water Lily"
102 "Fanny Crossfield"
103. "Fanny Crossfield"
104. "Ethel Jane" and "RGD"
105. "RGD" at St Ives
106. "Queen of the Chase" (NMMC)
107. Figurehead (Bosely Auctions)
108. "Sunbeam 2"
109. Original "Sunbeam" 1874
110. "Eugine Euginides"
111. Figutrehead.
112. "V.B. Lamb" off Treath
113. "V.B. Lamb" alongside lower quay
114. "Ryelands"
115. "Hispaniola"
116. "Pequod"
117. SS "Queen of the Fal 2"
118. Feathers
119. Swell Jumper
120. Granite Hammers
121. Bosahan Quarry Beta Engine (CM)
122 Bosahan Quarry Alpha engine (CM)
123. Hauling granite
124. Hauling Granite
125. Hauling Granite (Brian Spargo)
126. Wellington Monument (Brian Spargo)
127. Travelling derrick
128. Scotch Derrick
129 . Dressing shed

130. Scalping Iron
131. Freeman's yard, Penryn
132. 1842 Tithe Map (CRO)
133. Martyn's map1748 (CRO)
134. Greenwoods Map 1828 (CRO)
135. Ordnance drawing 1877 (CRO)
136. Ordnance map of Village 1878 (CRO)
137 Ordnance map 1908 (CRO)
138. Merthen Estate Map 1805
139. Brogden's Mine and Merry Meeting
140 Brogdens 1878Ordnance (CRO)
141. Polwheverel 1878 (CRO)
142. Polwheverel 1906 (CRO)
143. Merthen Estate map 1771, creek
144. Creek, 1805 , Merthen map
145. 1771, Lower Calamansack
146. Lower Calamansack 1852 (CRO)

Back Cover: Google Earth : Rounds and River

7

The Story of Port Navas

Introduction to 2nd edition

The first (1994) edition of this book arose virtually by accident . Whilst my husband Douglas and I were investigating the origins of our house, we unearthed a wealth of information about the neighbourhood and started assembling notes to create some sort of order. This led to a meeting with the local publisher Bob Acton, and the book developed. Since that time, a considerable volume of water has flowed under (and occasionally over) the bridge by the old Jolly Sailor pub. New knowledge has emerged, requiring corrections to some of the original text. The electronic age has arrived, and the village has evolved. Babies then yet to be born are now parents themselves while many of the old guard are no longer here. We are well into a new century, permitting two further census records to be released—up to 1911. In the original book, we began the story in medieval times, but in reality, of course, the beginning was very much earlier. It seemed like a good plan to write an update. Although some errors are inevitable, I hope there will be fewer in this account. Douglas sadly died in 1996, but I know he would have been fully involved in writing an up date. It was decided to stay with a size which fits most book shelves. The new edition should be a fitting tribute to his effort and enthusiasm.

I confess to having no Cornish birth rights, but in mitigation, I have known and loved the county since my first visit in 1929, aged 13. This followed the disappointment of a rained off Girl guides camp in Surrey. As consolation, my parents sent me on a train to stay with my uncle and aunt who were holidaying in Bideford. While there, I saw an advertisement for a Charabanc tour to Tintagel and Boscastle. Imagining an opportunity for close encounters with King Arthur, I booked a reservation for the next day. Reaching Cornish soil for the first time, a sense of magic developed. Choughs were flying on the cliff tops, and, whilst neither King Arthur, nor Merlin appeared, from that day on I was hooked.

 Cornwall became our family holiday destination throughout the 1930's. In those days it was a two day journey in the open Austin 12/4. My father was no mechanic, but the car never let us down. Falmouth was the normal choice, and a drive to the Lizard a regular annual treat. The route took us via Maenporth, through Mawnan Smith, Port Navas, Constantine, and Gweek.
Many things have changed since then, but equally, much remains the same. On the road west rising from the village centre at Port Navas, I well remember being amused by a house and tearoom with what, at first glance, appeared to be painted figureheads in the porch. In 1956 this same building came on the market, and became my home. 60 years later, I still live there, as do the figures in the porch. They are not ship's figureheads but statues.

The house was owned in 1930 by Graham and Helena Rogers, who also occupied a boat yard at the upper quay. In 1920, Graham had attended an auction at a Plymouth mansion, and made a successful bid for a collection of statues based on Grecian Goddesses. There were six. Presented with the challenge of transporting them home, the cheapest solution was the train. He bought six tickets , and they duly travelled with him back to Falmouth, which must have surprised fellow passengers. He sold three of his trophies on arrival, intending the remainder as a feature to lure customers for teas. They were never intended to be painted, but one figure, named by Graham "The Goddess of Plenty", had an exposed right breast! Mrs Rogers ran a respectable tearoom, and felt that her customers might be offended. In the interests of decency, the object had to be concealed. As I have said, Mr Rogers also ran a boat yard. A selection of left over boat paint was deployed to restore decorum, and thus the breast was duly painted. Alas! Far from discrete, it now stood out like a beacon. The only hope that nobody would notice was to paint the entire statue, and then of course the other two had to be made to match. If the original intention had been to attract interest, it certainly worked, because that is why the place remained so firmly imprinted in my memory. The statue painting tradition has stuck, but one has to keep abreast (pun intended) of the times. In this more liberal age, in line with the practice of some contemporary tabloid newspaper editors, the breast is returned to its fully exposed glory, for all to see! They make a useful landmark.

The Helford Estuary and Port Navas are greatly loved, and like much of Cornwall, are decreed "an Area of Outstanding Natural Beauty" (A.O.N.B). A number of factors combine to create beauty. Geology, climate, and human activity all play their part in the formation of a landscape. During the oscillating ice ages, sea levels have undergone dramatic ups and downs. 18,000 years ago, the coast was well west of the Scilly Isles, with Britain part of mainland Europe. Equally, raised beaches down river, left behind by previous interglacial periods bear witness to sea levels far higher than present. These would have completely drowned our present village.

Some 350 million years ago, movement of the earth's crust caused dramatic changes. Sediments deposited in a southern hemisphere ocean bed, were slowly but relentlessly, moved towards a northern continent. Some of the seabed rose over the land, creating the slatey rocks of the Helford River and Port Navas Creek. Further advance created enormous heat and pressure, resulting in the Lizard peninsular. Conveniently for us, the Lizard now provides a wonderful shelter from western storms. To the North of Port Navas, vast mountains appeared. Now eroded away, the huge blobs of granite at their base are at or near the surface. This material resource was the reason that our little Port was created. The resulting rocks also bore many metallic seams which became of huge economic importance to the region. Thus various characteristics created both beauty and enviable natural resources, ripe for human exploitation - good land and climate for crops, convenience of a sheltered shoreline for fishing , harbourage, and shipment of mineral bounty.

The opportunity to occupy an advantageous coastal spot offered an ideal lookout for contentious neighbours.

The local human story really goes back at least 10,000 years, to a time when coastal valleys were quite different. Mesolithic migratory hunter gatherers visited, leaving a few traces There are six Mesolithic finds within six miles of the village. Ancestral neighbours from so far back might seem irrelevant, but in the grand scheme of things, such time is nothing.

These ancestors would have experienced similar emotions, triumphs and disasters to those which we share today. They just lacked the benefits (or not) of modern technologies. They didn't endure traffic jams, strikes, power failures and computer crashes, because these things hadn't been invented. The weeks groceries were acquired without science, electronics and the world wide web. Life was unthinkably tough by modern standards, but these ancestors were in our part of Cornwall 10,000 years ago, and thrived! These people were the same human animal as ourselves, oblivious that they would later be classified stone, bronze or iron age. Our age is probably destined to be classified "The Electronic"!

By 6000 years ago, a "gabbroic" pottery clay was in nationwide supply and wide usage. It was all sourced from St Keverne. Whilst Bronze wasn't invented in Cornwall, tin and copper were discovered here. For that reason, our county and neighbourhood was in the vanguard of the metallurgical revolutions. A site at Coverack has revealed ceramics believed to be late Neolithic/ Bronze age. Goonhilly Down also has numerous Bronze age burial mounds, and bronze axes have been discovered at Durgan and Mawnan Smith. By the Iron age, even greater local evidence of human presence is suggested by the "Rounds" at Calamansack, Treviades, Trenarth, Drift , Treworval, and Goongillings. These were slightly fortified farming enclosures, usually in a round configuration. Within the enclosure were several round houses, which served as accommodation for either families or domestic animals. Two square enclosures at Merthen are thought to have had the same role, if somewhat more fortified, and recognised as a trading place for Romans. The farming community at Chysauster, above Penzance, points to an orderly civilised community. Through the Bronze and Iron ages, most communities were mostly agricultural , but shipbuilding and trading were needed. When the Romans occupied Britannis, many native Britons, migrated from the colonialists, and caused an increase in the Cornish population. Romans traded for the minerals produced by Britannic Celts, particularly their tin, but they do not appear to have taken over control of the mining and metallurgy, which remained with the local Celts. The Dumnonii tribe had not adopted money, which would have added an intriguing dimension to trading. (As in modern "we don't accept plastic"!).

The sheltered damp climate and fertile soil in Port Navas is, as gardeners know, highly conducive to growth. Neglect leads to a rapid return of forest environment.

Anglo Saxon relics here are sparse. Some Celtic crosses date from Saxon days. The name High Cross implies a religious gathering point from that time. Typically, High Crosses were tall with a carved cross on top. At our local spot so named, amongst several lumps of recently imported granit, the genuine cross was found in a nearby hedge, repaired and resurrected. It is believed to be 12th century. The name "Constantine" also comes from the Saxon period, but the settlement is far older. Archaeological evidence includes Neolithic and Roman finds. Some celtic folk shunned Saxon culture, and the Cornish population is again thought to have increased then as a result of migration from the east of the country. So after the Romans, for a second time the identity and culture of the Cornish Celts was reinforced. In the medieval period, larger farms and landholdings developed. In peak season a 100 acre estate would require at least 20 agricultural labourers, together with their families. An acre was rather loosely defined as the amount of land a man and horse could

1). I remembered the house with painted statues, from family drives in the 1930s. XR 2271 outside Pennance, 1931, returning from a drive to the Lizard. Our family car was an Austin Heavy 12/4 tourer. The journey from Wimbledon took two days at a maximum speed of 42 miles an hour, but it never broke down. I bought the house when it came on the market in 1956. (Image with thanks to Nicky Finan, courtesy of photoshop!)

plough in a day, however a Cornish acre, for no accountable reason, was 270 acres. Now there's contrary for you!

As well as food production, woodland management became an important local requirement. In the 18th and 19th centuries, bark for tannin was a key crop. Local ("Cornish, Irish, Welsh" Sessile Oak *quercus petrae*) was the favoured species for the process, and was selectively encouraged. Slightly different from the Common English oak, it survives better on rocky ground. The annual new growth bark was stripped from the trees, either whilst standing or by regular coppicing of the timber, and then boiled for its tannin, used in leather production and cloth preservation. The timber was used for building, firewood and faggots, and charcoal produced for tin smelting. This regular coppicing and pollarding results in rejuvenation, some trees living 5 times longer than normal, to well over 1000 years. It results in the stunted "scrub" oak woods which characterise the local landscape.

Our creek acquired the name "Cove" in the 18th century, almost certainly by the dwellers at Calamansack, which was mainly centred on the main river at Lower Calamansack. It was just a creek on the back of the estate. It is intriguing to imagine a picture of "Cove" before the granite wharves. Each of the estates shown inside the front cover included several cottages, of which few now survive. On the Calamansack side of the creek, some of Rose Hill dates to the 18th century, and newer houses stand on old cottage sites at Rose Cottage and Tire me out. The rear of Ponsaverran remains from the 17th century. The main track from Constantine is ancient, and little changed, as is the farm track ascending Trewince lane to Trenarth. Before building a quay road and quay, a few boats might have floated at the high tide. There may have been less mud prior to industrial detritus of the 18th and 19th century. Larger transport vessels could have been anchored down the creek. It would make sense that a cooperative of estates should run the bigger vessels, but such arrangements would depend on cordial relations among neighbours, most of whom were tenants and not owners.

Good evidence is lacking, but it is all food for thought.

Peggy Shepperd, February 2016

13

2. The geological setting of Port Navas   By Peter Scott

The bedrocks underlying Port Navas and the immediate surrounding area are mainly mudstones and sandstones and the Carnmenellis Granite (see map).

The mudstones and sandstones are sedimentary rocks belonging to the Portscatho and Mylor Slate Formations. They can be seen *in situ* in the wavecut platform and low cliffs of Port Navas Creek and the Helford River as well as in several cuttings beside the roads through the village. They were originally deposited as clay, silt and sand in a deep ocean basin approximately 383-359 million years ago, known as the Upper Devonian Period. During that time, there was a boundary, or suture, between two tectonic plates located in what is now the western English Channel, just south of the Cornish coast. The mudstones and sandstones represent sediment eroded from the landmass of the southern plate. The remnants of the plate now lie deep below younger sedimentary rocks offshore in Plymouth Bay. The two plates approached and collided, resulting in the loss of the intervening ocean. Some of the rocks of the Lizard, including the well known serpentine, are a fragment of those that were present beneath the ocean.

The plate collision resulted from the northwards movement of the southern landmass onto the northern plate. This formed what is known by geologists as the 'Variscan' mountain chain which, 300 million years or so ago, stretched across into much of Europe. By the time the collision finished, all of the Earth's continents were joined in a single landmass know as Pangaea. The plate collision resulted in the sedimentary rocks around Port Navas being buried, faulted, folded and heated up to just over 300°C, a process known as regional metamorphism. This caused some recrystallisation of the minerals in the rocks. A foliation or cleavage formed in the mudstones as they were squeezed, transforming them to slates, due to the alignment of minerals on a microscopic scale.

The planar (or slatey) structure resulting from the cleavage enables natural weathering and erosion of the slates to split or break them up into slabs, flattish boulders and smaller tabular pieces typical of the rocks on the beaches in the creek and shoreline around the Helford River. In rock exposures, the slates often have irregular veins of white quartz going through them and folding can be seen, although the dominant orientation is for the strata to dip steeply towards the south. This creates a weakness in the rock mass in this direction, which has occasionally given rise to small landslides where the steeply dipping rock is inclined directly towards the creek. The Mylor State Formation and the Portscatho Formation both extend eastwards to Falmouth and westwards to the coast around Porthleven. In the cliffs to the south of Porthleven, near Loe Bar, the zone of contact separating the formations and the differences between them can be distinguished. The Portscatho Formation is

SIMPLIFIED GEOLOGICAL MAP OF THE AREA AROUND PORT NAVAS SHOWING METAL MINES

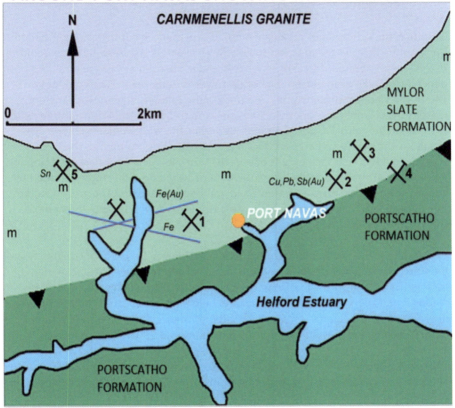

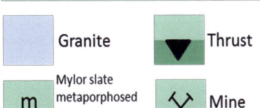

2. Geological map, based on Geological Survey, drawn by Nicky Finan

interpreted as having been thrust over the Mylor Slate Formation. In the area of Port Navas the contact is shown on the geological map to pass through the creek; but, the differences between the two formations are largely indistinguishable in the rock exposures, and the boundary between them is not recognisable.

Granite is the other major rock (see map). It is present in cuttings along the road to Constantine beyond the junction to Polwheveral and is also seen as large boulders in the steep 'mountain' stream that flows under the road at Polwheveral, the boulders having been eroded from higher up towards Ponjeravah. The contact between the slates and sandstones and the granite follows an east-west line approximately, from Trenarth Manor via Treviades and to the south of Constantine, with the granite being to the north. Granite underlies the whole of Constantine. The granite is the southern part of a very large intrusive body known as the Carmenellis Granite that has a surface extent of over 100 km^2. It is one of six large granite bodies and a few smaller ones beneath Devon, Cornwall and Scilly. Interpretation by geophysicists of the regional variation in gravity indicates that the granite bodies join up at depth making a huge elongate batholith, varying from 6-10 km or so thick, beneath South-west England.

The granite is the product of partial melting of older rocks, probably originally sedimentary, in the lower part of the Earth's crust at around 800-900°C. The melting took place towards the end of the 'Variscan' mountain building period. The resulting liquid accumulated in the crust and being more buoyant than the surrounding rocks moved upwards, emplacing itself into the Devonian sedimentary rocks, before cooling and crystallising as a granite at around 290 million years ago.

The granite is made up of crystals dominantly of the minerals quartz, alkali feldspar and plagioclase feldspar, with lesser amounts of muscovite and biotite mica, and some tourmaline. There are very small microscopic amounts of rarer minerals (<0.01%) including apatite, sphene, zircon and some other minerals containing uranium and thorium. The radiogenic decay of the uranium and thorium minerals gives rise to radon gas that can accumulate in buildings both above and adjacent to the granite, including in the houses of Port Navas.

Two types of small vertical or sub-vertical intrusions, or dykes, cut through the slates and siltstone in a few places in and around Port Navas. One is a pale coloured granite like rock called felsite or elvan on older geological maps. The second is a darker rock called lamprophyre, which is indirectly related to basalt. All of these intrusions are only a few metres wide at most and are probably a few million years younger than the granite. They are more common than those marked on Geological Survey Map as thess shows only those exposed or otherwise discovered during the time that the geological survey was made. In addition, small dykes of granite can be found immediately adjacent to the main granite body.

In geological terms, the slates are said to have been "hornfelsed". New minerals can form in slates that have been metamorphosed in this way. Very occasionally boulders of slate in the fields and streams around Port Navas can be found containing elongate crystals of the mineral andalusite. This is a characteristic mineral of slates that have been heated by being adjacent to a granite intrusion. The area of metamorphism caused by the granite intrusion extends over most of Port Navas, including the Bosaneth Valley, Polwheveral and Nancenoy, but not Calamansack.

Superficial sediments that formed only in the recent geological past (a few thousand to less than two million years ago) occur on top of the bedrock. They include alluvium made up of clay, sand and pebbles eroded from the bedrock and deposited in the river valleys, as well as the mud and other sediment in Port Navas Creek, and the soils.

The chemical weathering and physical breakdown of the bedrock makes up the major component of the soils in and around the village. Small boulders of slate, sometimes permeated by irregular veins of white quartz, and sandstone are often brought to the surface by ploughing in the arable fields of Calamansack and between Trewince Lane and Trenarth. In a few places the soils are underlain by a jumbled mass of irregular shattered slates, known to geologists as 'head'. This can be seen in some road cuttings and in the low cliffs on the south side of the upper parts of the Creek. It is the product of frost action during the colder periods of the Ice Ages (around 11,000 to 1.8 million years ago), when Cornwall had a tundra landscape. Cobbles and boulders of granite, often stained red or brown, can be seen in the soils above the granite.

The most recent geological history of Port Navas includes the development of the creek and the sediments it contains. It is well known that the Helford River is a ria. This is a drowned river valley, the original valley of the Helford and its tributary creeks being inundated by the sea as the level rose after the last ice age. The original and deeper Helford River and its tributaries had already formed well before the ice age by preferential weathering and erosion over millions of years of the more susceptible parts of the Portscatho and Mylor Slate Formations. Apart from the central channel and the pebbly beaches, the bed of Port Navas Creek is a thick layer of silty mud, rich in organic matter (decaying leaves, twigs and other vegetation) up to two metres thick in places. The mud is underlain by a pebbly sandy clayey layer, which probably is sediment deposited when the rivers were much more active immediately after the ice age, although some coarse sediment could have been brought into the creek from the Helford River as the sea level rose. The more recent mud is derived largely from the erosion of soil that is brought down by the river that feeds into the creek at the slipway in the centre of the village and by the rivers at Anna Maria and Trenarth Bridge. This erosive process is very evident when the water in the creek turns a chocolate brown after heavy rain.

17

3). The Mylor Slate Formation dipping steeply towards Port Navas creek

4). Carmenellis Granite in cutting beside road to Constantine, showing more horizontal jointing towards the ground surface

Further reading and study:

Geology of Britain Viewer: http//www.bgs.ac.uk/data/mapViewer/home/html

The Geology of Cornwall. University of Exeter Press, 298pp Silverwood, E.B.,Durrance, E.M. and Bristow, C.M. (1998)

Cornwall's geology and scenary (2nd edition). Bristow. C.M. , Cornish Hillside Publications, St Austell, Cornwall. 167pp (2004)

3.Pre History

Modern humans first appeared in North East Africa around 200,000 years ago[1], but since the end of the last ice age, our species has spread and prospered more than in any previous interglacial period.

The Historic Environment Record[2] and "ARCHI" database[3] each catalogue significant archaeological finds throughout the UK. During the 1990's, and since the first edition of this book, Cornwall County Council sponsored extensive aerial searches for sites in the county. In 2000, the Cornwall Archaeological Unit published a historic audit of the Helford estuary[4]. All these activities have provided much greater information and understanding of this area in prehistory, as far back as 8000 B.C.

In 2015, within 6 miles of the centre of Port Navas, 321 recorded archaeological finds are recorded dating from Mesolithic to Medieval periods . Of these, 20% are Bronze age (3,300 to 1200 B.C.), 40% are iron age (1000 BC to 400 A.D), and about 8% Roman (53 to 410 A.D.). The remainder are medieval, stone age or unspecified. There are 7 Mesolithic and 2 Neolithic sites, dating from up to 10,000 years ago. At that time, warming global temperatures during the preceding 2000 years had caused rapid thawing of arctic ice. This accelerated when the North American lake broke out of its ice dam. Fresh water flowing onto the surface of the North Atlantic submerged the (heavier) salty Gulf Stream, and conditions reverted to cold for more than 500 years. This period is known as the "Younger Dryas"[5]. The "Western approaches" between Cornwall and Brittany was a gulf about 65 miles wide. Land bridges joined Dover and Calais, Guernsey and France. The nearest local coast was about 3 miles east of the Helford river mouth. Vegetation was largely Birch and Pine, in fairly open terrain. This was the environment when hunting Mesolithic groups first visited. Flint axes at Falmouth and Zoar may have been employed for shaping wood, and

5). *The climate and flora 10,000 years ago were like North Canada*

arrow heads were bound to hand held spears. More concentrated finds are between Porthoustock and Coverack, which was then well inland, some 150 ft above sea level, and a promontory overlooking the coast. These people were migrant hunters, unlike the Neolithic and later settlers who made permanent homes.

As the weather warmed, Oak and Hazel forest replaced the former pine and birch, and forest canopies became increasingly dense. The bleak Goonhilly down was easier to deal with and probably explains why the Lizard

6). *Creek head as it might have appeared at high tide in 400 B.C*

peninsular has a particularly high concentration of Neolithic and Bronze age artefacts[6]. It suggests a denser population in that area. Trade was surprisingly widespread. Stone tools and "Gabbroic" pottery clays from St Keverne were traded or transported throughout Southern England[7]. This is because pottery made from this unique material was found to tolerate heat from a fire[7]. To date, Cornwall has the second highest concentration of Neolithic archaeological finds after Wiltshire. Creation of permanent homesteads needed enormous human endeavour, particularly in protected valleys where vegetation is prolific. There are two early Bronze age barrow finds, and 66 later Bronze age sites in our neighbourhood. These include barrows on Rosemullion head, Constantine, two at Drift farm above Trenarth and at Treviades. A significant population of tribal residents were working the ground (unaware they were to be labelled "Bronze age people"). The tin industry also provided trade. It may have been exported from Helford, although only West Penwith is mentioned by the Greek geographer, Diodorus Siculus in 400 B.C.[8] (chapter 7) But it is the iron age inhabitants who dominate the archaeological record in Cornwall. They established farm enclosures, usually in the shape of a "round". Bigger enterprises than their Neolithic and Bronze age forbears, even more forest clearance would have been necessary. They achieved extensive grazing for livestock, and tillable soil for crops. Several enclosed rounds survive as fields (Back cover). Some of these are actually in Port Navas– at Calamansack, Treviades, and High Cross. This perhaps could be considered a time when the village vaguely acquired an identity and community. In 400 B.C., high tides were 4 feet lower than today[9], but the accumulations of silt (Port Navas mud!) was less, and navigable water was probably better than present. Farmstead "Rounds" were usually sited on high ground. Since the Calamansack finds are so near to the village centre, it is appropriate to focus on that area. There are three separate probable rounds, possibly all contemporary. The most obvious is an eighty yard diameter site on the field brow above Calamansack wood which borders the west bank of Abraham's Bosom which has been recognised since 1868[10]. (picture 7). Adjacent to this enclosure is another probable round of similar size but perhaps older, with field systems outside the compound. At Lower Calamansack is a further possible round and field system.

At Merthen, adjacent to a medieval deer park, are two square enclosures with surrounding fields. Some have suggested this is a Roman fort, but the majority archaeological view is they are well fortified "Rounds" which happen to be square, in a prominent position, with a fine view down the river[11]. The location was probably an important Roman trading post. Two hoards of Roman coins and treasure have been found in Constantine[2], and another opposite Trengilly Wartha Inn. These Celtic folk had no currency, and would not have needed Roman coins. Whether the above mentioned coin hoards were placed by Romans or local traders remains open to speculation.

There was significant metal production throughout Cornwall, probably from 3000 years ago. In the vicinity of Helford, tin and copper predominated, both essential in the continued demand for Bronze. It is clear that the Romans traded with the local Celts (Dumnonii tribe), but the colonialists did not apparently take over the production processes, which was left with the indigenous people[12].

What would life have been like growing up in "Port Navas" 2000 years ago? It is a mistake to underestimate people , and the local residents of that time possessed many skills identifiable with the present.Most of our local predecessors were agricultural, little influenced by national politics or innovation. Working the land was gruelling. The "proto" plough was called the ard. Either pulled by a draft animal, or pushed by men, its stone (and later iron) tip scratched the ground to create a tilth. Iron age livestock included horses, oxen, sheep, goats and pigs. And, of course, man's best friend, dogs. Two and four wheeled carts were available. Accommodation was in a thatched round house. Sizes varied from 3 to 40 metres diameter[13]. In the house was a central fire, with smoke exiting through the thatch. The fire provided heat, cooking, and some lighting. A kitchen area was located to one side, and sleeping on another. Raised beds were mattressed with straw. All generations were conceived, born, lived, slept, and died (much younger than today) in this home. It all looks rather cosy, but the aroma would have been interesting if hard to imagine. These accommodations would have been present within the compounds of all the iron age round sites locally. There is a true iron age fort on Denis head, but our immediate village enclosures were designed to confine livestock when necessary, rather than defence against aggressors. The arrangement likely varied little over 2000 years. In an estuarine location, fish and molluscs would have been an obvious source of food, but skeletal isotope evidence from Bradford University suggests that it was not favoured in our country from 6000 B.C. until the arrival of the Romans. An early irrational dietary fad? Roman occupation caused westerly migration of native Britons, who preferred to retain the Celtic languages and culture. The Cornish population increased in the Romano British period. A trackway said to be of Roman period runs from the old port at Maenporth, above our village, to Polwheveral, through Merthen woods to Gweek[13]. The "new" 1572 bridge at Polwheveral contains material from a Roman period structure which was upstream.

After 500 A.D., there is a dramatic decline in archaeological finds.[14] There are no Anglo Saxon discoveries within our 6 miles radius. Saxon farmers introduced the mould board plough, which required long field lengths to reduce the protracted turning manoeuvre. Strip fields characterised the Anglo Saxon agricultural development of the Mould Board plough. In Cornwall, survival of so many small fields suggests that the faithful ard remained in common use in our neighbourhood, with more economical oxen as draft.. The old Brittanic Celtic language was modified to Cornish. Both observations suggest that the Anglo Saxon culture failed to penetrate this far West. The Anglo Saxon Chronicle records numerous conflicts between the Cornish and English through the 6th to 8th centuries. A Cornish / Danish alliance culminated in defeat by King Egbert of Wessex at Hingston Down near Callington in 836.[15]The boundary of Anglo Saxon Wessex and Celtic Cornwall was set as the Tamar.

By the time of Domesday, only Penryn (Trelivel) gains a mention. Presumably the way of life continued much as before in the Iron age.[16]
The Dumnonii tribe occupied the territory from Exeter west, and persisted as the local "Kingdom" throughout Iron age, Roman and early Saxon periods, a span of over 1500 years. Although they traded metals, these people had no currency. Why all the Roman hoards ?

References

1. Stringer, C. (2012). "What makes a modern human". Nature 485
2 . Cornwall and Scilly Historic Environment Record
3. ARCHI UK
4. Helford Estuary Historic Audit. Cornish Archaeological Unit, 2000
5. Hunter gatherer behaviour in the younger dryas. Metin Erin
6. LAN (Lizard Ancient Sites Network)
7. Gabbroic clay sources in Cornwall: a petrographic study of prehistoric pottery and clay samples. Lucy harrad 2004
8. Laing, L. R. : "A Greek tin trade with Cornwall" in: Cornish Archaeology; 7, 1968, pp 15–22.
9. Archaeology of the Moors, Downs Heaths and OFWest Cornwall Peter Dudley, 2008
10. Helford Esturary Historic Audit , 2000
11. History of Constantine, Henderson & Doble, 1937 P89
12. A book of Cornwall. (London : Methuen, [1906]) Baring-Gould, Sabine
13. The Roman Road through Constantine. Peter Bale Constantine History Group
14. ARCHI Database
15. Oxford Index. A search and discovery gateway. 2000
16. Domesday for Cornwall

7). Google earth view of the creek. oyster farm and quays (upper right). The crop mark in the field is one of three Calamansack rounds. It measures 100 yards diameter, and would have accommodated approximately 40 people plus their domestic animals. Likely date is 300 B.C.

8). Life in the Round 2,400 years ago. Tilled fields are outside the compound, but most livestock is kept within. Conventional domestic animals include horses, cows, sheep, pigs, chickens, and dogs. The small field has been tilled with an ard.(courtesy Fran Stuart)

9). Iron age round house. Each of these would have accommodated up to 15 people in our enclosures. Round houses varied from 3 to 15 metres diameter. The central fire provided heat, cooking facility, a little light in the dark, and smoke. No chimneys, the smoke exited through the thatch in the apex. By fortune, the smoky atmosphere controlled insects and bacteria. Scene depicts, clockwise from 2 o'clock, a) man operating "ard", b) man turning earthenware pot, with gabbroic clay, c) man forging iron on an open fire, d) skin drying on stretching frame, e) girl feeding a lamb, e) girl collecting water (courtesy Fran Stuart).

10). Above. Reconstruction on original foundations in Castell Henlys.

4. Medieval Manors. and Farms.

This account is moderately detailed on the basis that interested readers will be frustrated by omissions . The definitive sources are wonderfully summarised by Charles Henderson's History of the Parish of Constantine. An Oxford Don, he died in 1932 age 32, and it was published posthumously in 1937. This book remains the gold standard data source. It is highly recommended reading[1.] Constantine parish register and Vestry books are also invaluable.

 The Port Navas valley watercourse runs from High Cross towards the creek head, roughly bisecting the road to Constantine and Trewince lane. It gains a second stream from Calamansack hill beside the village hall. As in chapter 3, evidence suggests that the land around has been farmed continuously since Neolithic times. 6th century Cornwall had at least one (and possibly several) Dumnonian Kings Constantine. Tintagel is thought to have been of Royal importance in the Constantine dynasty[2]. King Constantine was criticised for behavioural issues, involving murdering his opponents. Subsequently reformed and sanctified, he was, in legend, a successor to King Arthur. Also he provided the name of our Parish church and village. The early Saxon period, from 500 A.D. is likely to have seen only gradual development from the preceding Romano British lifestyle, and would have closely resembled the appearance 1500 years previously. Nothing much changed. The prefix "Tre" prefix (homestead) is associated with middle and late Saxon holdings[3]. Such names as Trenarth, Treviades, Treworval, Trewince and so on, are used in the earliest records, and it is safe to assume the Saxon connection. Anglo Saxon culture saw the introduction of "Feudalism". Because the Celtic lifestyle buffered the Saxon rulers, stubborn resisters of the new order migrated west. Cornwall is believed to have become more populated in those so called dark ages, as a result of this migration (like the 21st century in Europe). Domesday (1087)is a record of Saxon holding, and names no local manors apart from Breage[4], but this is because the bailiffed or tenanted farms ("Bartons") were owned by more remote "Super Manors". In our case, this was Winnianton, which encompassed an area in the South half of the county from Porthleven, west of the Lizard, to Mylor. Of our local farms, only Trewince is named in Domesday. Later Trewince was an estate farm under Trenarth Barton. By late medieval times, there were five principal estates, and three small farms which abutted, enjoying access to the creek head at "Cove".   Our Bartons were Trenarth, Treviades, Inow, Calamansac and, Ponsaverran, as follows:

Trenarth. Early records[5] show it was owned by the "Trenerth" family, who would have taken their name from the estate, rather than vice versa. Richard Trenerth is mentioned in a 1260 document. They held it for many generations until the early 16th century, when it was acquired by the Crane family of Camborne. An undocumented story is told, that the Cranes had won the estate in a game of cards. In chancery proceedings of 1515-25[6] a suit is recorded by Thomas Trenerth, brought against the Cranes, concerning lands in Trenarth, Trewyns and Penrevren, recently owned

26

by Jenkyn Trenerth, the plaintiff's uncle. Presumably he won the case, because the Trenerths returned as residents from about 1540. This could be a pointer to the game of cards story, In 1660, another James Trenerth died, and his daughter Anne gained the inheritance. She married Henry Trefusis of Mylor, who already owned Treviades. So both estates came under the absentee Trefusis family. But when her husband died, Anne gave the Trenarth estate to her son, who did become the resident. He in turn died in the early 18th century, which seems to be when it was acquired by the Nicholas family. This exchange of ownership may be from where the card game rumour stems. The Nicholas family retained ownership for four generations, latterly leasing it[7]. They developed the house (see below) and the estate. It appears likely that the Nicholas's installed the estate gates at the three access points to the farm—one at the approach lane from High Cross, one at Trenarth bridge, and one at the lower end of Trewince lane (a second gate at the top of this lane marks the boundary, after the Rev James Mayne bought Trewince farm in 1884). Although the six foot high gates are long gone (were they wrought iron?), the granite posts survive in situ, and may be seen. A family named Reed were tenants in the early 19th century. One of the progeny, a Joseph Reed (b 1823) emigrated to Australia, and became a key architect in the development of Melbourne[8]. The estate was sold in 1842, when it came into the possession of a Mr Magor, who did

Trenarth
11). Top: 1930s 18th century front.
12)..Above. 1930s .Mrs Trerice with Medlyn meat waggon, and pig.
13). Right: Rear courtyard by Tom Cross

didn't live there. In 1880, John Boaden bought Trenarth for his sons to farm[9]. This clan held a seat on the Lizard Peninsular, and had other holdings. Local son John Boaden was involved with the New Wesleyan Chapel project of the 1890's. He presided at the opening ceremony. He died in 1903, and the farm passed through various ownerships. By the 1930's, the Trerice family supplemented income by accommodating paying guests. (chapter 12 the Harrisons). The Clarks ran a B&B in the 1950s. Currently it is thankfully in the caring ownership of Lucie Nottingham.

The beautiful and imposing farmhouse for Trenarth comprises several stages of construction. The front is elegant Georgian, built by the second generation Thomas Nicholas in the late 18th century. Behind this is the original house now acting as the kitchen, with an Elizabethan courtyard, all built about 1560. This back part of the present house has a doorway (original front door) with the Trefusis /Trenerth combined shield in a lead plaque dated 1658. The same crest is on Ann Trefusis's (died 1692) memorial in Constantine church. None of the medieval building is left.

Treviades Manor. This estate is also first recorded in the 13th century[10], when the resident lord was Baldwin de Treviados, who held it from the Duke of Cornwall as overlord. It remained under this family for possibly five generations, until one Joan de Treviados, daughter of a James, gained the inheritance. This lady married Peter de Trefusis of Mylor, which was when Treviades became part of the Trefusis estates (As above). The smooth talking Trefusis clan had a habit of marrying well, and developed an enormous number of estates, but remained based in Mylor. The Black death hit in 1349, when no less than 9 members of the local land owning society died, including Peter and Ann Trefusis. In the chaos of the plague time, it appears that Treviades, Iccombe, Polwheverel, Trewince and Inow were retained in occupation by a number of families who presumably had already held the tenancy. But there was nobody collecting rent. At a special assizes court of 1410, the ownership is re established with Richard Trefusis[11]. The family held Treviades for 20 generations, until Lord Clinton sold off many local properties after WW 1 . A Thomas Trefusis became resident in 1590 until he died in 1645, and probably built the granite Manor house. His family lived in Constantine parish. One of his sons , Richard, held Iccombe. Treviades Barton House is a very attractive original 16th century manor, built around a courtyard, with three sides of the house, and a wall closing the fourth in an 18th century remodelling. **Trewince** farm as mentioned above as a separate Barton in Domesday, had become part of Treviades. The farmyard buildings of the 18th century and later period survive two thirds of the way up Trewince Lane on the left. As mentioned, this track was one of three accesses to Trenarth. In the court Rolls for Treviades of 1613, James Trenerth is described as "Holding Trewyns as a free tenant of Treviades manor, rendering a Red Rose annually with 18d and suit of Court and a relief of 6/3d"[12]. Assuming this is the same James whose daughter Anne married Henry Trefusis, it may explain the point at which Trewince became part of Trenarth, which owned that farm in 1820. As above, Treviades also owned two other farms which no longer survive, Iccomb Wartha (Higher) and

28

Iccomb Wollas (Lower). Iccomb is first recorded in 1327, and divided by 1649[13,14]. Both farms were accessed from the main lane up to Treviades and High Cross. They were absorbed into Treviades after 1851. Iccomb Wollas was on the right of the lane opposite the silage pit owned by Treviades farm. Masonry stone is occasionally found there from the old farmhouse. Iccomb Wartha was located further up the hill, and was a free tenement for the Richard Trefusis (above) where its former wide gateway offers a stunning view of the Port Navas valley . The farmhouse stood on the opposite side of the road above a high bank, where some trees now stand. A spring pours water onto the lane in wet weather, and this same spring provided water for the house. The boundaries can still be identified. The last census return naming residents for these holdings is 1851, and the buildings were demolished presumably soon after. Their land is now part of Treviades farm.

Inow . The settlement of Inow is first recorded in 1269.when it is spelt 'Iwenau'. The name is Cornish and possibly contains the element hiuin meaning yew- trees. It was ransacked in 1530 when owned by John Arundell.[15] It became a part of the Merthen estate, and a Vivyan property. Originally one tenanted farm, by the 1842 Tithe map, it has been split into two separate holdings, apparently due to a mar-riage settlement of 1825. The bigger share was owned by the Trefusis family, per-haps associated with their other holdings in the area. Henry Collins now farms a total of 250 acres. On the wall outside Pennance is a stone with V and T inscribed— the boundary between Vyvyan owned Calamansack and Trefusis owned Inow.

Calamansack . As in the previous chapter, this estate boasts three probable iron age rounds. The settlement clearly existed in Saxon times, but the first record (referring to the woods) is in 1249 when it is spelt 'Kylmonsec' [16]. The name is Cor-nish and contains the element 'Kyl' meaning 'nook' or 'back', and an unknown ele-ment 'Monsec'. Subdivided in the C14th into Higher Calamansack which represents the original iron age settlement, and Lower Calamansack which represents the lat-eral settlement. Lower Calamansack is first recorded in 1463 as 'Kylmonsec Woles' (Woles = Wollas=Lower)[17]. This was the most densely populated part of our village area in the 18th and early 19th century, when the Mayns dominated. In the 1841 census, 50 people were living at Lower Calamansack, which had 136 acres. In the same census, Higher Calamansack has 112 acres, with two farmhouses and four-teen cottages. Higher Calamansack borders onto the estate woods at Abraham's Bosom, Pill Creek and "Cove" creek, where three estate cottages had fruit gardens running down to the water. The name "Cove" makes particular sense for a commu-nity occupying this hill, which also borders onto the Helford at Lower Calamansack. Cove was almost certainly merely a location in that estate.
The documented descent is complicated by marriage settlements, most families remaining absentees. Take a cold towel to follow the sequence!
Owners for several generations were the powerful Alet family, descended from an Algor, Lord of Edelet mentioned in the Domesday book[18]. In the 14th century,

ownership was shared through marriage of the last Alet daughters, by two clans named Durant and Hamley. In the fifteenth century, a Durant heiress, Joan, married Sir John Arundel of Trerice, which line thus acquired part title. Another Devon family called Fortescue with whom they had recurring spats also had part ownership. Thus Calamansack was passed by marriage through several families, most of them absentees. By 1621 it was leased by James Trenerth of Trenarth.[19] By 1649, Calamansack Wartha was owned by Sir Richard Vivyan, and rented to Sir Vyell Vivyan[20]. By 1842, the then Sir Richard Vivyan owned Calamnsack Wartha, and half of Calamnsack Wollas with Francis Rashleigh. Hence the above mentioned boundary stone!

Ponsaverran. As mentioned, this estate was first recorded as "Penreveran", and was part of Trenarth lands in 1327[21]. Situated on the headland headland above our main creek, the Pen prefix may refer to this. It appears to have been bought from James Trenerth in 1649 by Walter Kestell of Manaccan, who developed the estate[22]. An interesting tale relates to him. His wife bore him no son. Determined to secure the estate in his family name, he approached a Hannibal Kestell of Egloshayle, who was unrelated. He persuaded Hannibal to marry his daughter Avis, promising the estate would go to them unless Walter had a son. Shortly after, his wife died and he married her young maid, who presented him with a daughter and a male heir, John. So sadly, Hannibal and Avis lost out, and returned to Egloshayle. The Kestells probably built the original house, (which was partially destroyed by fire in 1870, Chapter 5) chapter). The Kestells remained absentee landlords, unlike the Mayns who followed in 1780.

At this point, it is perhaps worth visiting the conflicting theories and debates over both the name and location of Port Navas. In the lease to Walter Kestell in 1649 Penreveran has become Porhanaves, and in 1729 Porranaves. Henderson interprets these as meaning Porth an Hewas "Harbour of the Summer abode". The Historic Audit appears to make a case for the name Port Navas being a corruption of Ponsaverran, but in the 1813 ordinance map, both names are recorded- "Ponsaverran" appears, with "Port Navas" immediately above Inow. For many generations the creek head was known as "Cove", and continued with the same name in the census returns throughout the 19th century, but this name does not appear on any maps. The exact name Port Navas coincides with the arrival of the Mayns, and possibly indicates their aspiration for developing a new port. James Mayn may have provided information on names to the ordnance surveyors . His interest in purchasing Ponsaverran estate is conventionally thought to have been its oyster farming potential, but it is possible there was always a plan to develop a port. Port or Porth, and Navas or Navis appear to be mere spelling whims. The original drafting of the first Cornish Ordnance map was in 1801, when James Mayn's sons would have been managing the old man's affairs and estates (James was 68 that year). The small backwater of Cove was ripe/vulnerable for development, and just maybe the ambitious Jonathan fed a new name to His Majesty's surveyor, with vague similarities to his Ponsaverran estate.

Budock Vean. Although now in Mawnan Parish, and the other side of the creek from our village, it was previously part of Constantine[23]. Budock Vean is an adjacent holding of 250 acres, and warrants inclusion. The settlement of Budock Vean is first recorded in 1327 when it is spelt "Sanctus Budocus"[24]. The name is taken from that of a Cornish saint plus the element byghan meaning 'small' or 'little' . On the 1748 Martyn map (Appendix C), what is now Port Navas creek is named Chielow. ((Leland 1538 = Cheilow). William Borlase published a text on the area in 1758, and names our creek as "Chielow, alias Calamansack"[25,26,27]. Richard Chaylow held Budock Vean in the 14th Century. Rose Hill cottage was formally Chielow. Sally Thomas tells us that in recent times the name has been applied to the main creek beyond the Oyster Farm, to the head at Anna Maria. It was owned by the Pender family from the 18th to the 20th century. On the 1758 map, the owner is Pender Esq. Benjamin Pender became one of the twelve men of the parish vestry book. His grandson, William was a wealthy attorney, who married Anna Maria Peters in 1825. They had 4 children. He died in 1850, leaving Anna Maria as the widow matriarch for 20 years. She owned and developed the eponymous copper mine. When she died in 1869, the estate went to her oldest son William Rous Pender, also a solicitor. The mine was neglected for 30 years, but reopened briefly in 1907 (Chapter 7). It is now a renowned hotel and golf course.

Merthen, Polwheveral, Nancenoy and Goongillings.

These fascinating neighbouring estates deserve a book in their own right. Hopefully a few anecdotes will not go amiss. **Merthen** was in Royal ownership since late Saxon times. From 1408 it became seat of the Reskymer family [31]. They created the deer park adjacent to the fortified rounds (of square formation) mentioned in the last chapter. In 1629[32] it was bought by the Vyvyan of Trelowarren. Their main residence however remained Trelowarren, and Merthen was mostly leased, although later some family branches took up occupaton. The Tyacke family held the lease throughout the 19th century. The old part of the lovely house dates to around 1575.

Being in the southern sector of Constantine, the surrounding hamlets have had a significant influence on our village through time. The track running from Treviades, crossing the Constantine road and on to Polwheveral and Nancenoy, is early medieval or prehistoric (chapter 3). The section from Treviades to the Bridge was called Clodgy Lane[28], possibly meaning Leper house or "embanked". From its top end, bronze age barrows lie in the field to the right. The lane is cut well into the hillside, and runs steep after crossing the Constantine Road, to the "new" bridge. The Bridge over the stream at Polwheveral was built in 1572 by Roger Hallard, for Constantine Parish, recycling some of the previous Roman period materials. It was widened later. Here, Polwheveral was divided (at the bridge), into Wollas and Wartha (now Goongillings). In this narrow shortcut to Gweek, traffic jams and delays often occur. In the untanglement that ensues, put aside frustration. Just relax and absorb the antiquity of the location! As described in the next chapter, the Mayns leased

Polwheveral Wollas. This part was owned by Lord Trefusis of Treviades. The Mayns leased it for several generations in the 16th and 17th centuries, and ran a small cloth manufacturing operation. The community were engaged in fishing, farming, weaving, and tucking. Water mills are recorded there in16th century Treviades survey. There were two grist mills for corn, and a fulling mill, run by the Mayn family. Fulling is a process of cleaning and beating woven cloth in order to "flannel" the product. Also called "Tucking" as in Tucking and Weaving. Later the stream drove a wheel operating bellows for the blow house (now lower Goongillings Cottage). This was used for smelting tin from Wheal Caroline. All of Polwheveral was part of the Manor of Trewardreva[29], which was owned and held for many generations by the Trewrens. Mary Ann Trewren married a lawyer, Charles Scott in1818, who then acquired the estate. Their daughter Caroline gave the name to the eponymous mine (chapter 7). Goongillings was formerly Polwheveral Wartha. Charles Scott gave his name to the wood and also developed the first Scott's quay[30]. This original quay was (and still is) 15 metres out from the present structure, nearer the deep water channel. Like Jonathan Mayn's enterprise, it was intended for granite shipment, and may have preceded the Port Navas developments. There would undoubtedly have been rivalry between Charles Scott and Jonathan Mayn, living on the opposite bank. This part of Polwheveral (Wollas) was leased to Treviades, opposite at Lower Calamansack. The quay conspicuous at the beach is newer, built in the late 19th century and restored in the 1930's. It was also tidied in the 1960's, when the royal family enjoyed a picnic there after a trip up river in the Royal Barge from Britannia which was moored in the river mouth.

To the west of the track to Scott's quay, further pre historic artefacts are present in Merthen woods - three Bronze age Barrows, and another Iron age round.

The estate came under the Trelawarren Vyvyans after the mid 19th century.

The farming / fishing community at Nancenoy , a part of Merthen, was also owned by the 1733 James Mayne of Port Navas.

Trengilly, This farm is mentioned in a recovery of 1 acre of land in 1286,and a conveyance of the entire holding in 1337 [34] . It comprised two parcels, namely a Veor (Wartha) of 45 acres and a Vean (Wollas) of 39 acres. It was originally a small farm of just over 80 acres, and part of the Carwythenac Manor, which itself was subjugated by Merthen[33]. It was held in lease by John Reskymer of Merthen in 1588 under the Tremaynes of Carwythenack. The farmer of Trengilly Wollas in 1851, was a Benjamin Bawden. The Dunstan family still farm at Nancenoy, and this family name is traceable locally to the 16th century. The Victorian farm cottages of Trengilly Wartha may have become a beer house (Kiddleywink) and then became licenced in 1960. It is now a great success, under the excellent guardianship of Will and Lisa Lee. It has been voted West Country Pub of the year, 1st choice in trip advisor, and gained national recognition as runner up for CAMRA pub of the year, and likewise for best breakfast. Modestly it is described as "Probably the Second Best Pub in the Country". Arguably it is clear winner on points, and is a great tribute to the dedicated team running it. We are lucky. Perhaps it should be awarded Manorial Status?

References

1. Henderson History of Constantine (HHOC)
2. Pearce, Susan . "The Traditions of the Royal King-List of Dumnoia" (1971).
3. HHOC
4. Domesday Cornwall
5. Daily Life in Arthurian Britain. Deborah J. Shepherd
6. Chancery equity suits before 1558 - The National Archives
7. The Medieval Account Books of the Mercers of London: An Edition and Translation. Lisa Jefferson
8. Reed, Joseph (1823–1890). David Saunders
9. Magor Conveyance CRO
10. Crown plea roll, 1283., 111 Baldwin de Trviades witnesses a deed, estimated 1280 . National Records
11. Obit Kalendar of Cornish families 14th century, copied in 16th century by Chiverton (Henderson0
12. 1613 court rolls
13. Rental of Manor of Treviades, 1613. CRO
14. Henderson History of Constantine, p 188
15. Star Chamber Proceedings, Henry 8th , 3, 140 NRO
16. Ibid no 123
17. White Book of Cornwall, 1356.Ibid
18. Cornish feet of fines, No 3
19. Chancery proceedings 1515-1525. British Library
20. The Royalty of Helford River and Oysterage.(HHOC, 110)
21. Chancery Proceedings 1515-1525. British Lbrary
22. Vivians Visitations, 1874, p.484
23. Chiverton Obits , MS. At Shute, Axminster
24. Rental of the Manor of Penryn Foreign. 1538
25. Leland 1538. Cheilow,
26. Martyn 1750 Chielow.
27. Borlase 1756
28. Survey of Treviades Estate,1649
29. HHOC, 77– 81
30. HHOC, 77
31. Charter Rolls 1236. Confirming exchange of Merethyn by Richard, Earl of Cornwall to Gervase of Horningcote
32. Deed of settlement, Arundell Carminow inheritance 1395
33. Ancient Deeds of Merthen Manor, PRO
34. HHOC
35. Trengilly Wartha website.

5. The Mayns of Ponsaverran

The Mayn presence at Ponsaverran dominated the evolution of Port Navas throughout the 19th century, and laid the foundations of our village today. Dr William Boxer Mayne (1876-1955) was a GP in Swindon, and great grandson of the James Mayn who bought Ponsaverran in 1780. He recorded a history of his family in 1950 as an in house document, and this is an invaluable source of information on the Mayns/Maynes[1] (The two spellings apply to the same clan!).

Unlike the Vyvyan and Trefusis owned estates, this family were never "absentee landlords", but always locals, dating from the middle ages. From the 18th century, they held both Lower Calamansack—originally the main local centre of population, and Ponsaverran which enjoyed extensive frontage onto Chielow creek and Cove.

The Mayns were a respected local family, thought to have originated at Maen Pol and Maen Pern farms north of Constantine. For, several generations in the 17th and 18th centuries, they occupied Polwheveral as tenants from Treviades. As in chapter 4, they ran a fulling mill powered by the stream which passes down the valley. They were described variously as fullers, tuckers and farmers. Cloth making was labour intensive. Spinning and weaving in those day were entirely a cottage industries, but the local community were dependant on the Mayn fulling service. The Mayns also farmed and fished—presumably sheep for the wool. They had frequent disputes with the Vyvyans over fishing rights, but eventually were given permission to use "ground sayn nets" up river from a line connecting Maen Broth (a local landmark rock just below Frenchman's creek) and Calamansack bar. Their catches were mainly Pollock, Whiting and Mullet, for local consumption. In the early seventeenth century, some Mayn descendants had land at Calamansack for drying nets (and again, later, farming). In 1572, the Vestry book for Constantine Parish records that Symon Meane, unable to pay his rates, "was delivered one heifer, all white, at half store, stock and increase for the term of eight years if the said Symon Mean dwell so long in this parish, and if he do depart, to re-deliver it up again." This would seem to have been a charitable deed, allowing him to breed some stock. Within two years, Symon was sufficiently afloat to pay the rates. In 1695, a John Mayn, yeoman of Constantine died in debt of £200 to Exeter creditors —a significant amount.

It is the 18th century Mayns who principally concern the Port Navas story. 30 years after acquiring Ponsaverran, England was in the middle of the "Industrial Revolution", which resulted in such dramatic changes to the British way of life. The country was in conflict with Napoleon, and the Peninsular war was raging. Steam power was in ascendancy, and Cornish engineers were pioneering its application in mining, creating a heavy local demand for coal. By 1820, McAdam's roads began to transform land transport. Stagecoaches could average a previously unimaginable 12 miles an hour, but heavy commodities, such as granite, coal and grain still required shipment by sea. Large civil engineering projects developed, and demand for granite took off.

Male Christian names often perpetuated through generations, making the descent a little hard to follow. So hold on!

James Mayn , of Lower Calamansack born in 1727 was the man who bought Ponsaverran from the Kestells. It may have been an opportunist purchase. The Kestells lived in Manaccan, and had to supervise this small farm from across the river. It is generally believed that the principal Mayn interest was the water frontage, in order to develop oyster beds in the creek, away from the restrictions placed by the Vyvyans of Trelowarren. As suggested before, this James Mayn may have contrived the name Port Navas.

When he died at Ponsaverran aged 87 in 1814, he left a considerable estate . He had acquired a number of properties—freehold at Nancenoy and Ruan Minor, and leasehold at Polwheveral and Stithians.[2] He likely accumulated the bulk of his finances from the Oyster fishery. Long before trains, oyster sales could have only been for local consumption. But Falmouth was expanding at the time, and oysters were a staple food. Ponsaverran and Calamansack were inherited by his son and heir Jonathan.(1762—1835). Jonathan continued fishing and farming at Calamansack. The third oldest son William (1797) took up the residence and farm at Ponsaverran .   It seems very likely that transportation of granite commenced at Cove creek head around the turn of the 18th century. This would have involved vessels taking the ground, and loading from waggons on the beach. With a mostly downhill run from Carmenellis quarry, the waggoners would have favoured the much shorter journey, rather than hauling to Penryn. But a poor track from Constantine, and the soft shingle foreshore were obstacles. For trading vessels, the amenity had serious short-comings. As above, **Jonathan Mayn** was born in 1762 . He would have been acting as his father's right hand man from soon after the acquisition of Ponsaverran, and he was the prime mover in developing the village which endures to this day . He married Jane Boulder of Constantine in 1782.

A contemporary description recounts "He was a man of medium build, fair in earlier life, eyes blue and rather deep set, with bushy eyebrows. Clean

TO STONE CONTRACTORS.

TO BE LET BY TENDER, for 7 or 14 years, a new built GRANITE QUAY, 200 feet long, situate at Porthnavas, Parish of *Constantine*, in Helford Harbour, and in the immediate vicinity of the principal Granite districts.   The above QUAY is built for the express purpose of Shipping Stone, having a fine road to and from the different quarries, and nearly all down hill.

TENDERS will be received by JONATHAN MAYN, of Constantine aforesaid, till the 20th of May next, after which the Person whose Tender is accepted will have due notice thereof.

April 29th, 1830.

14). *Jonathan Mayn's advert, Royal Cornwall Gazette 01.05.1830. If 200ft includes the three sides with water frontage, it suggests two stages of building the upper quay.*

haven except for small side whiskers, sharp in face with a somewhat prominent nose. In character, while being eminently business like, he was of a lively disposition, and believed in enjoying life. At the same time, he clearly had a generous nature, was a good neighbour. Having sown his own crops, he was ever ready to send his workforce and horses to assist a neighbour who was behind with his work. Jonathan Mayn appears to have had both abundant energy, and great vision. Perhaps a Poldark like character. It was of course he who drove the major investment in Port Navas, upgrading the road from Constantine, building a track alongside the steep and uninhabited North bank of the Cove, and constructing a large quay to which vessels might come alongside, specifically for the granite trade. What chance he would get it through planning today?

Stone for the abutting wall on the quay road required hauling and dressing in the days before the industry was properly established locally. It is constructed with granite piers made from 12" by 12" by 24" blocks, double thickness laid with sequential courses perpendicular to its neighbour. The capping course is of 18" blocks. The piers are on eight yard centres, and the infill is carefully laid slate stone. It is a remarkable tribute to the masons and engineers involved that there has been negligible subsidence or need for repair in nearly 200 years, despite constant heavy traffic. Jonathan also had built ,on the quay road, a seamen's chapel and rest room no doubt to make the port attractive to mariners, and a lime kiln , for processing chalk cargoes brought in from the eastern channel ports by vessels shipping out with granite. (The chapel is now called "Mayn Cottage", with JJ Mayn inscribed on the wall, the initials of Jonathan and his wife Jane) . He also built a beer house in the

15). Above left: Calamansack Farmhouse, built by Jonathan Mayn (1759-1835). He lived there with his wife Jane. His second son James followed . The annual lime feast was held in "the Long Room" there.
16). Right: Scribings cellar wall depicting 14 commercial sailing vessels. Courtesy of Mrs Helen Collins

17). Left, "JONATHAN MAYN A.D 1832", and Right, ordnance ledger mark, cut into the granite blocks on lower Calamansack quay.

village. Small beer sales of "home brew" were quite common in this part of Cornwall, the establishments known as Kiddleywinks. The pub may have been one of these initially. In the 1841 census it is called the Sailor (later "Jolly" Sailor) so it was clearly aimed at marine clientele. This original premises is the double fronted cottage which adjoins the late Victorian extension with hung slate upper elevation, now called "Chestnut". Simultaneous with the Port Navas venture, Jonathan upgraded Lower Calamansack, developing the waterfront with a revetting wall and quay, a net drying stand and a fish salting house. He also built a substantial new house there for himself. His name is engraved in granite on the strand at Lower Calamansack. His prime interest was the sea, both fishing and yachting. As early as 1824, he was advertising a 24 ton new built yacht for sale. There are many wonderful exciting tales about Jonathan. On one occasion he was delivering home a new three masted lugger from Plymouth, when heavy weather came in off the Dodman. They were lucky to survive, but managed to beach the vessel at Portscatho. The boat was subsequently christened "Providence". Another occasion, Jonathan's second eldest son William was working the Oyster beds in the river when he was approached by a press gang, and abducted at the point of a blunderbuss. From there he was taken to a naval frigate anchored in Falmouth bay. On learning what had occurred, Jonathan immediately sailed out and boarded the frigate, demanding to see the Captain. After an undisclosed dialogue, William was released. But there must have been a risk that Jonathan himself could have been detained. Where would Port Navas now be had that occurred? Another press gang visited Lower Calamansack in search of a particular villager. The man was hidden in a bedroom chimney breast, and a four poster bed placed against the wall in front. When the Gang arrived to inspect, Jonathan's wife Jane climbed into the bed, feigning severe illness. They departed empty handed. On a further occasion, Jonathan and Sir Vyell Vyvyan were sailing together. Sir Vyell , who was described as "apt at times to be peculiar in his head", suddenly turned and exclaimed to Jonathan "One of us must jump overboard, Mr Mayn", to which the reply came "Then it must be yourself, Sir Vyell". The conversation was rapidly dropped. He held an annual "lime feast" in the long room of his new house at Lower Calamansack, when he collected the dues owing from local users of lime he had provided. The feast was free, but it was an effective way of rounding up late payers.

Jonathan's oldest son (also Jonathan) established a ship victualling service in Flushing. On visiting there one day, father Jonathan encountered several old salts lounging about on the quay. When told they were retired, he exclaimed "If it were me, rather than do nothing, I would go fishing, even if I had to throw the catch back in the sea".

Jonathan died in 1835 aged 73, only 5 years after completion of his various building projects. In his will [3], he left £20,000 (£2,000,000 in todays money). His wife Jane, four sons and two daughters survived him and were the beneficiaries. Son Jonathan (1793) appears to have been considered established and independent. He received no part of the estate, and only a £30 annual allowance (30,000 today). 5 years after his father died, he went bankrupt, but later became a partner with an uncle James in the oyster business, and eventually moved to Mylor. James(1796) the religious second son, (and father of the Rev James below) continued farming at Lower Calamansack. William (1797) the third oldest son, by arrangement with his brothers, inherited Ponsaverran and continued to run it. He thereby supervised the wharf at Cove. He became Swedish and Norwegian consul, perhaps through Scandinavian connections in shipping, and also undertook the collection of data for the 1851 census. He owned the quay, and instigated the building project for the second quay, which was only just completed by the time he died in 1865. Ponsaverran was inherited by Williams sons, but both were engaged as parish priests, and the estate was next occupied by the youngest brother, Josiah (1802). Known as Captain Joe, he had farmed at Calamansack but also remained in the oyster trade, having beds in Mylor. William's twin sister Mary Ann became widowed, and moved in with her brother Captain Joe at Ponsaverran. In 1878, when Mary Ann died, her body was laid out in the bedroom, while Captain Joe and his wife went to Falmouth to make arrangements for the funeral. In their absence, Ponsaverran burned down. During the inferno, the corpse had to be handled out of a window and placed in the stable. The house had to be rebuilt. The original walls were retained, and a large new front was added, with a new roof which is seemingly pitched at right angles to the original. During Captain Joe's tenure, the water course was retrained through the village, bridging the stream by the pub, where previously had been a ford . The pub was modernised, with the large slate hung extension mentioned above. This was on re ground regained from the redirected stream (Chapter 9). Joe himself died in 1883 aged 80. His brother William's two Vicar sons still owned the estate through their inheritance, but were fully engaged in their parishes. It was bought then from them by their cousin, the Reverend James Mayn, who had conducted Josiah's funeral. It may be that an agreement was reached at that family gathering , when all the cousins were present. At the time, the Rev James was vicar of Romansleigh in Devon, and also private chaplain to Sir Thomas Acland, a Tory, then Liberal MP. Being the oldest son of the religious James of Lower Calamansack, the Rev James had been born in the village, (see above) and was the great grandson of the original Ponsaverranowner James Mayn. Lower Calamansack had been sold, but he had inherited Bufton farm in Constantine. He had been curate of Constantine, and married Emily Jane Hosken of Penryn, whose granite merchant father was first to lease the Quay in 1831 (chapter 6).Emily Jane died in 1863, when their daughter Catherine was 6, and he re married, to Ellen Marsden, who came from a wealthy Manchester family. James and Ellen had one son, Ambrose. This James Mayne clearly had a great commitment to Port Navas, and his arrival brought various benefits to the village. The rebuilt Ponsaverran was considerably bigger, with better amenities. He arranged for the road from Ponsaverran towards Mawnan to be re routed towards the creek, less steep than its previous route which went in any case went through the farmyard at Ponsaverran. (Traces of the original route survive). The new road was donated to

38

the village on the occasion of Queen Victoria's golden Jubilee in 1887. He also bought parts of Trenarth, including land at Trenarth Bridge and Trewince farm. When the Rev Mayne died in 1897, the estate passed to his only son, Ambrose (Amby). He was a close friend of John Seager, the schoolmaster at Ponjaravah, and organist at Constantine church. John was the son of an army officer, and had grown up and trained in St Thomas, Devon. It is possible he had met the Maynes previously . Such was Ambrose's friendship, that Trewince house was built in 1893 for the Seager family, on land bought from Trenarth[4]. In the event, the Seager family of six moved into Ponsaverran, which had far more space than Ambrose required for himself. The Seagers effectively became his surrogate family. Ambrose retained a bedroom and study. Allegedly, Ambrose had been ordained. He never sought a parish, although he regularly read the lesson at Constantine church, where John Seager continued as organist. Mr Seager gave up his teaching, and by the 1911 census is described as "estate manager". He lived as a funded gentleman at Ponsaverran, and is included as "gentry" in Kelly's directory. His daughter Muriel married Thomas Webber in 1916. Thomas, like his father before him, was an ex mayor of Falmouth. He was also Chairman of Falmouth Corporation Oyster Fishery. Their original family business became the Baker's Oven. In 1932, he was ordained as a priest and became lay preacher at Constantine, then curate at Liskeard, and finally vicar of Lostwithiel from 1935 to 1947. Thomas and Muriel's son Philip was godson to Ambrose, who used to read bedtime stories to his young charge at Ponsaverran. By some accounts, Amby was a little unusual. He invested in, amongst other things, the Great Western Railway, but was not an astute business man, and faced financial challenges. Quite frequently, he visited Romansleigh where he had grown up. He never married, was a keen chess player and avid reader. Sally and Robin Thomas remember him with affection, and his hobby of catching butterflies. So does his godson, Phillip Mayne Webber. John Seager's second daughter married a Captain Frank Honey, who came from Essex as business manager for the Oyster Farm. He built the original Dinyan bungalow from timber. n 1926, Frank commissioned a valuation of the Ponsaverran estate. This document survives and contains interesting communityl details, as does the updated version after Ambrose Maynes death at Ponsaverran in 1941 aged 72. The Maynes were no longer represented at Port Navas. In his will of 1928, Ponsaverran estate was left to Thomas Webber, and the residue to the Rev Edward Seager, John Seager's son. John Seager stayed on at Ponsaverran until 1947, when he moved in with the Webbers in Lostwithiel. He died in 1954. Ponsaverran was let to a succession of tenants, most notably for 10 years, John Coats of the Cotton Empire. He ran a charity called "Wings of Friendship", supporting orphaned children of any country following World War 2. Ponsaverran became a vacation break destination for these children. Subsequently it had a period as a hotel, run latterly by Brian and Dotty Roper, and then a phase when it became rented flats. In 2004 it was restored to a beautiful country home by Philip and Margot Webber, who continue to reside there.

References

1. William Boxer Mayne. Unpublished document.
2. Will of James Mayn 1815. National Records Office
3. Will of Jonathan Mayn 1835. National Records office
4. Conveyance Boaden to Mayne, 1890 CRO

41

6. A fledgling Port Navas and the Granite Trade.

Granite is a common igneous rock often exposed on the surface of continental land, usually only appearing by erosion of the overlying rock deposits. In South West England, the "Cornubian Batholith" (granite rib) is the core of an eroded mountain chain (see chapter 2). This runs from Dartmoor to West of the Scilly Isles[1], and surfaces in six main areas including the Scillies. Our local Carmenellis was the biggest commercial producer of building stones and other granite products[2]. The durability of the material has been known and exploited throughout the ages covered in this book, with many bronze age menhirs, saxon (and more ancient) celtic crosses, and Medieval buildings. It became of a considerable economic value, particularly in the 19th century. Surface "Moorstones" were the original source—large local examples being Maen Tol, Maen Pol and Maen Pern. Following the industrial revolution, huge projects arose, and granite demand exploded. It became necessary to quarry for granite stock, and this quarried material was also better quality, being free of weathering[3]. By the end of the 18th century, consignments were shipped from the beach at Goongillings, and almost certainly the creek head at Cove, including for the first Waterloo bridge. A rapidly expanding road systems caused massive demand for kerbing, and the construction industry had an insatiable appetite. All this required phenomenal human effort. Finished stones varied in specification. For such structures as a lighthouse, very fine jointing tolerances were required.

18). A granite gang at Bosahan Quarry about 1910. Notice the swell jumpers with central ball weight (4 in the picture). Stout tripod work stand (name and purpose not known). Post crane, background right, see appendix B.

The commercial side of the industry worked as follows:

Building developers put out tenders for material from stone "buyers". The buyers would negotiate a price with the quarry owner for a particular consignment. The quarry owner employed several "gangs" working under a "ganger". The ganger in turn negotiated with the owner a sum for working a block, and the money received was divided out among the gang at agreed rates. This was known as "piecework". It was a good system for most parties, with virtually no speculative investment involved, but fluctuating rate of trade was a drawback. In lean months, the men depended on savings which barely existed, and feeding the family was a struggle. Constantine quarries included Retallack, Maen Pern and Maen Tol, Tresahor, Bosahan, Trewardreva, Trevase, Treculliacks, Callevan, Treglidgewith, Carvedras, Job's Water, Lestraynes and Trewoon. Also at Brill , Tremayne and Borease.

Splitting the stone at the quarry involved drilling a series of holes using a "Swell Jumper". This was a long rod tipped with a hardened iron at each end, and a weight in the middle which acted as an impact hammer (Appendix B). Bessemer's invention of steel permitted more durable tools. The tips were ground to achieve a cutting edge, with two bevelled faces. The edge later had a forged hardened insert . The operating technique was two strikes and turn. On average, 131 strikes achieved a 3" hole. The method is now replaced by pneumatic tools. Holes were spaced about three inches apart, along the line of the required split, and the these were then fitted with two metal "feathers", with a wedge between them. Striking a row of wedges and feathers caused cleavage of the stone. Another method was to drive in wooden pegs, which were then wetted, causing the pegs to expand. After 1860, blasting with gunpowder was also employed. The rough stone was dressed with stone chisels until it was smooth enough to use. All quarries and dressing yards required a blacksmith's shop for forgings, sharpening and repair.

The next obstacle was transportation. The stone had to be loaded into heavy carrier waggons, and taken to a port for shipment—an additional challenge requiring great responsibility and experience. Carriage of these massively heavy blocks from quarry to the port required a six or eight horse team. The waggons carried drag chain anchors for control down the hills. Penryn wharves could accommodate larger vessels alongside, and ship heavier blocks.(Appendix B). For some local quarries this had required an arduous six or seven mile haul to Penryn. There was surely much jubilation at Jonathan Mayn's enterprise in Port Navas - half the distance, on good roads, and mostly downhill. The new wharf would be usable at neap as well as springs tides. The creekside road required a the wall along the north bank, backfilling with slate rubble to create the track. It was designed for tide water to flow into the backfill and out again, similar to the method employed by the Dutchmen who built Falmouth and Flushing, (chapter 5), The builders clearly found firm foundations, because the structure remains perfectly solid, with no repairs showing, as good now as the day it opened 185 years ago.

Richard Hosken, aged 34, a local quarry owner, took the first 25 year lease. Larger vessels began calling at the new port in 1830, ballasted with coal or chalk. The character of old Cove was transformed, and destined to become increasingly busy over the next 70 years.   Navigation would have been challenging for wind powered vessels, involving warping and kedging. There may have been less silt, but maintaining the channel would be a constant challenge. The images overleaf give some indication.

So what was it like for the visiting mariners? There were no dwellings on the quay road, just the Lime Kiln next to the Chapel, and a non resident entrance hut. Once ashore, not a lot went on . The prayer room (now Mayn Cottage) provided a daily service on the upper floor, while a rest room below , which apparently offered a hot meal. The Sailor Inn (owned by the Mayns) had a brew house and a skittle alley, and was trading soon after the quay was finished. James Uden is recorded as landlord in the 1841 census. The original building may have been constructed before the quay opened. Jonathan Mayn only lived another five years, and his son William likely instigated much of the early developments.

By 1840, three cottages were located at the creek head. "Croft" the newest is still there, "Rose" cottage and "Pope's" are replaced. Two other small dwellings, "Tire Me Out" and "Rosehill" were on the Calamansack bank, with cottage gardens and fruit trees, all part of Higher Calamansack farm. Ponsaverran, the only substantial house, was out of view on the hill above the quay. A single cottage was opposite Inow, opposite Inow farm entrance on the road to Constantinee. However, judging by the marriage records, the village seems to have had representation from Cupid and his bow. for visiting sailors. Many local girls became sailor's wives.
Coincident with the early years of the new port, a London granite merchant, John Freeman and his two sons, had won a contract to supply material for the new Naval basin for steam ships at Keyham in Plymouth harbour [4] (which finally opened in 1864). They were therefore looking to establish a base in the granite area of Cornwall. Affairs at the head office in Millbank were left to one son, whilst the other older son, John, travelled the country to source suppliers. With the substantial quantities required for the dock contract, he decided to purchase his own Cornish quarries, and run them himself on the lines set out above. Richard Hosken, who had the lease on Port Navas quay, was the only other significant local business in the trade. The two firms appeared to work in collaboration for many years. Richard also had wharves at Penryn where he lived, on Quay Hill. His daughter married the Reverend James Mayn, who had grown up at Lower Calamansack and much later owned Ponsaverran (chapter 4). John Freeman also acquired a quay at Penryn near the swing bridge, so Hosken's and Freeman's became neighbouring businesses. Richard Hosken concentrated his business in Penryn. His son William traded independently in timber and other building materials, and Richard gradually

relinquished quarries to Freeman's. In 1856, he did not renew the 25 year lease on Port Navas Quay, which then went to Freeman's, who owned 80 quarries and became the biggest firm by a large margin. Richard Hosken continued trading until he died in 1867 aged 71, when his son William took over. The firm merged with Freeman when William died in 1906. Bearing in mind Richard Hosken's date of death, he is wrongly blamed for ordering destruction of the Tolmen Stone on March 9th, 1869! This huge moorstone was at Maen Tol quarry, then owned by the Hoskens. People came from miles to see this much prized artefact, Mwhich measured 33 ft. diameter, 97 ft. circumference, and weighed 750 tons, It also had religious connotations. It sat on two supporting boulders, enabling a man to crawl beneath it, an act the Druids believed purified the soul. (Borlase). On the date above, a series of charges blew it into fragments. A huge furore erupted, questions were asked in Parliament, and "the Builder" published an article in 1877 describing it as an act of vandalism. But the damage was irrevocable. William Hosken announced that it had been a danger. He wrote to the builder, elaborating the circumstance. The antiquity had been offered to archaeologists by his father some years previously for £200 (a tenth of its granite stock, value) with free access—finished material then was about two pounds ten shillings per ton). The archaeologists declined. The quarry foreman ganger, who allegedly had strict instructions not to touch the rock, blasted the

19). Maen Tol photographed before its destruction in 1869 (chapter 6). Handy for purifying the soul by crawling underneath. The Mayn clan is thought to have derived their name from the adjacent farm

20). "Lady of Avenel" loading stone alongside the upper quay, said to be 1875 when she was a year old, but she wasn't converted to barquentine rig (as here) until 1877 following damage in her first commissioned year. She went on to become quite famous. The figurehead survives in Germany , and the binnacle in Poole. (see appendix A).   Note the Scotch Derrick, with wooden treads on its Samson post, facilitating service / clearing of the swivel and top block. The crane jib is pointing up the creek, towards the roof of Rose Cottage. Gantry for the overhead crane in the background. This image and 21). indicate the extent of silting. "Lady of Avenel" drew 9ft laden, and she appears to be aground, about 2ft above her marks, with 6 courses of the quay wall showing. Her keel is thus on the bottom about 14ft below the quay top. This lower wharf at the upper quay appears to be of later construction.

Notice the roof of "Tire Me Out" (then home to John Rendle) underneath the bowsprit. It looks thatched. Also "Rose Cottage" - building on sky line under the Scotch crane spars, and roof of Pope's cottage, extreme right..
Possibly the most valuable image in the book, - oh for the original glass plate to improve quality!

21). 60 years later, in 1936. The Scotch Derrick is no longer present. Three masted topsail schooner "Fanny Crossfield" is discharging coal in the same berth. She drew 9ft 10in, and her keel is probably resting 15 ft. below the capping on the quay. This is about 4 ft. less today, but the ship's weight plus dredging would create a hole. The mud bank in mid creek is thought to be dug spoil from clearing the wharf edge. Still present, it may now be a tad bigger. Bunny Thomas's graphic artist father, mother and brother, plus dog are sitting on the wall for the slipway to the half tide quay. This view of the upper quay is now obscured by a ramp to the pontoon berths.

22). Below . View from the quay, of the same vessel. (See appendix A) Cart collecting coal, which was sold by weight. The habit of leaving coal to be covered by the tide at lower quay would have adversely affected the scales. Iron frame for travelling lift still present, but the Scotch derrick has gone. No problem departing after discharging a cargo, but arrival in ballast to ship out a full load of granite would be a different matter! The channel needed constant maintenance. Note Rose Hill ahead of mainmast.

foundations by night, claiming that the massive stone restricted operations, and was unstable, endangering his men. The Tolmen Stone incident was used politically as an argument for the protracted bill for Protection of Ancient Monuments (passed 1888). It is now remembered by Constantine's. Tolmen centre.

Building the lower quay at Port Navas was as big an undertaking as the original development. The track needed to be extended, and again an abutment wall was required. It was opened in 1865, soon before the death of William Mayne. It is not clear how it was funded, but the quays remained in the Mayne family ownership. The new quay had a large "Scotch derrick" type crane, with a mast, boom and stays, similar to that at the upper quay seen in photographs in this text. The locating hole for the mast is still visible. The upper quay also received upgraded facilities at this time, including a similar derrick. It had previously been served by a mobile gantry running on paired rails—one mounted on the wall abutting the quay lane (which still survives), and the second parallel mounted on vertical iron posts nearer the quay entrance. Tackle from the vessels rig would have been required in order to swing the granite into the hold. A further addition after Freemans took the lease was the construction of a shed for dressing the stone before shipment, a new Blacksmiths shop between the prayer room (Mayn cottage) and the lime kiln , and an office in the end of Mayn. Soon after these improvements, a tied house (Now Plumtree Cottage) was built to accommodate a resident quay master. The quay master in 1881 was Walter Humphrey, but there is no one holding the position in 1891. Shame we can't find a ledger book!

An entry in Lane's Guide[5] to the Helford River of 1891 describes Port Navas as:

"This busy little port, having granite wharves and quays of considerable size, with cranes and derricks for the loading of large blocks of granite from the Constantine quarries. Immense numbers of these blocks are piled up forty or fifty feet high, waiting to be loaded into two or three ketches, schooners and smacks moored under the cranes or anchored in the stream".

In 1880 when silting in Penryn became an issue, Freemans told Penryn Harbour Board that Port Navas had deeper water[6]. The Western Daily Mercury of 01.06.1868 reported "there were three gangs of men (stevedores), at Penryn, and two at Port Navas". The heydays of Port Navas as a port were in the 1870's and 80's. In correspondence to the Rev James Mayn from Freeman and Sons in 1889, the best year in the early 1870's had seen 3,657 tons shipped, and the worst year 1258 tons. (Penryn peaked at 30,000 tons).

Iron ore from Brogden (Chapter 7) would have added a further 2,000 tons of annual freight (chapter 7). Assuming an average cargo of 90 tons, the busiest year would have seen more than 60 ships through the port. Over 70 years, maybe 3,000 vessels used Port Navas. The volume would have been greater in the summer and autumn, winter months being unfavourable for coastal vessels. Likely two ships per week through the summer months. Continued correspondences from Freemans to

The Rev James Mayne makes a submission for reducing the rent on the quay[7]. Freemans argue that the cost of shipment from Port Navas is 4 pence (old money) greater per ton than from Penryn, based on pilotage down the river, towage as required, and a reluctance of skippers to navigate up the muddy creek. There is , perhaps selectively, no apparent mention of the savings in road haulage! Nevertheless, trading conditions were clearly increasingly challenging—mostly because Scandinavian suppliers were undercutting the market. Having renewed the lease in 1890, Freemans pulled out of Port Navas 9 years later.

Some notable contracts receiving granite from Constantine quarries include: Smeaton's Eddystone Lighthouse of 1756. He chose Treglidgwith granite for the building. Circumstantially it would likely have been shipped from Cove. When replaced in 1877, it was re erected on Plymouth Hoe, where it remains today. Rennie's Waterloo Bridge (1808) almost certainly included Moorstones shipped from Cove before the quay. Other projects included Rennie's London Bridge 1836 (now in Lake Havasu City California), Railton's Nelson Column (1845) , Woolwich Steam Dockyard (1851) , Baker and Son's Keyham steam basin(1850), Shaw & Shaw's Ramsgate Harbour (1850), Chatham Dockyard refurbishment(1862) , Barry Docks (1889) and Tower Bridge (1894), although most of the granite cladding for this iron structure came from Cheesering on Bodmin Moor.

John Freeman was a highly respected boss, and evidently a gentleman. His letters in the correspondence above are at all times courteous and reasonable. When he retired in 1872 his employees (about 600 of them), marched from Penryn Station past his house to the Polytechnic hall, led by the Constantine Silver band. Spontaneous or coerced? The story of the Freemans is well documented by Peter Stainier in several publications, and includes a list of supply contracts. Penryn remained the bigger operation. After refinancing, and amalgamations with competitors McLeod's in 1936, the Freemans continued at Penryn until 1973. Hoskens also continued in to the 20th Century, amalgamating with Freeman on the death of William Hosken. A block of granite remains on the lower quay to this day, awaiting its customer. There should be a preservation order on it! The foundations for the derricks are still identifiable, and the quays remain remarkably sound- a tribute to the commitment and endeavours of their builders.

Sadly, however, cheaper foreign supplies of granite fulfil the market requirements, beside the conversion to much cheaper reinforced concrete as the principal construction material.

References

1. The Tectonics of Variscan Magnetism of South West England. Le Boutier
2. South West Granite. Peter Stanier (recommended further reading)
3. The Story of british Granite, Ewan Hyslop and Graham Lott
4. The Battleship Builders. Constructing and Arming British Capital Ships. Ian Buxtom, Ian Johnston
5. Lane's Guide to the Helford river, 1891. CRO
6. Falmouth Packet, February 4th 2016
7. Correspondence between J Freeman and J. Mayne, 1889-93

7. Mining

Definitions for the unfamiliar:

Lode. An ore that fills a fissure or vein in a rock formation.
Shaft. A vertical excavation for accessing a lode. Access was required for men and machinery, and removal of quarried material, ventilation and pumping out water.
Adit. A nearly horizontal passage or tunnel leading into a mine as for shaft above.
Stamping Mill. Water wheel (usually "overshot" in Cornwall) driving a series of hammers to crush the raw rock.
Blowing House. Is for smelting ore to white tin. Air is pumped to the furnace, creating a higher temperature. The air is provided by waterwheel driven bellows.

It used to be said that, where a hole is found anywhere in the world, there will be a Cornishman at the bottom of it. The Camborne School of Mines, formed in 1888, is a world leading institution[1], based on expertise evolved from the industry.
Mining has been in Cornwall since early times– possibly 2150 BC.
The Greek geographer, Diodorus Siculus wrote in 400 B.C. [2]
"The inhabitants of that part of Pretannis (Britain) called Belerion (Land's End), from their intercourse with foreign merchants, are civilised in their manner of life. They prepare the tin, working very carefully the earth in which it is produced . Here then the merchants buy the tin from the natives and carry it over to Gaul, and after travelling overland for about thirty days, they finally bring their loads on horses to the mouth of the Rhône".

A massive 75 kg tin ingot, thought to be of this period, was recovered from the sea bed in St Mawes harbour in 1812 , whilst dredging for sand (Baigree 1983)[3]. In addition to archaeological evidence, there are numerous references to mining, and smelting of tin and copper through the Iron age and Romano British periods [4]. The Domesday book has no reference to tin in Cornwall. In the 12th century, the biggest production was in Dartmoor. Mainly this was found by streaming, although open cast mining may have appeared in prehistoric times. When the Devon area was worked out, Cornish production dominated. In the 14th century, Cornwall peak production was 650 tons and by 1400 had risen to 800 tons[5]. There were tin booms in the 16th and 18th century, by when Newcomen atmospheric engines were a major advance over manual bailing. But the hey day came with the introduction of Trevithic steam engines in the 19th century. At its zenith 600 beam engines were working mines in the county.

All the local mines were on private land, and leased by the mining Adventurers" (speculators). The business arrangement for a mining venture was to attract shareholders, who provided the investment for equipment and construction for operating the mine. It was always a gamble! The owner would often be a shareholder.

Major mine operators locally included the Vivians, Fox's, Brogdens and Freeman's (of granite fame). Most adventurers had a broad based portfolio of shares in a number of mines. In a Vivian study of 60 copper mines reported in 1800, only 13 were profitable[6]. Steam power dramatically improved the returns. In our immediate vicinity, there were three substantial mines and two smaller operations, with lodes of copper, tin and iron. (See map, chapter 2). Most of the miners came from Constantine or Wendron, where mining was more intense. In the 1861 census, there is only one tin miner living in Port Navas, named Richard Rowling

"Brogden Iron Mine", also called Inow Mine, went down to 60 fathoms. The three main shafts and site of the portable engine are opposite the junction of Treviades lane and the Constantine Road, adjacent to Calamansack gate. The field beside this cross road has always been called "Merry meeting" (Appendix C). There were also adits entering directly from the field below.

It was worked from around 1865 to 1875. Maximum production was in the early 1870's. Several iron miners are recorded living in Port Navas in the 1871 census. A report that year describes a seam of good quality haematite being worked by Messrs Brogden, a local Falmouth branch of a family engaged in Iron mining throughout the UK. The company became insolvent in 1884.
According to "Metalliferous Mining Region of South West England"[6], the ore had 50% metal content, and in 1873 alone, sold 2000 tons. There was a stamping mill at Ponjeravah, and this may have serviced production rock before shipment. It would

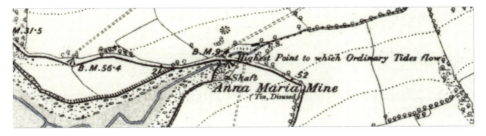

23). Ordnance maps : 1878 (above), and 1906 (below). The lode was copper. In 1906, new adventurers engaged contractors to re open the mine. Sometimes HM surveyor made errors. It was never a tin mine!

be strange if the ore were not shipped from Port Navas, with a quay just

24). Construction workers and miners, Wheal Anna Maria, 1907.
25). Below. Anna Maria Mine, 1907, from the land side, looking South. Engine and its shaft on the West side, planned down to 30 fathoms at this stage. Allegedly it leaked 3,000 gallons in 24 hours of both fresh and sea water, making it uneconomic. The Copper and Gold are still there!

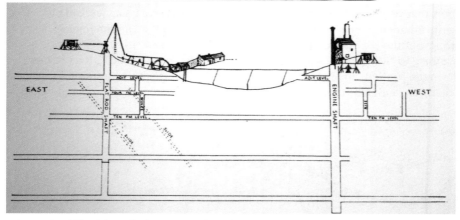

down the hill, although there is no firm documentation. Storm water at the site still stains brown with iron oxides.

"Wheal" means place of work, and not mine. The **"Wheal Vyvyan Mine"** was in Constantine, and far the biggest local mine[7]. It was on the road to Trebarvah, at the back of the now closed Ruberry's Garage. The lode was tin and copper ore, and ran 6.2 degrees south east and dropped 4 ft. in every fathom. In the 1851 Grace's guide[8], it is leased from Sir Richard Vyvyan of Trelowarren. The purser was a William Carne, and the captain James Bryant. Offices were on the mine, which was worked from 1827 through to 1864. There were 80 men employed, and the ore was shipped from Gweek.

Above Trenarth bridge, on the left of Bosaneth lane, there was a small copper mine in the valley called **"Wheal Bosaneth".**, which appears to have been worked in the late 18th and early 19th century. It lay 100 yards south of "Roskellan" which was the captain's house[9]. Two adits were driven eastwards from the stream with a shaft adjacent. It is thought that these were intended to bisect with lodes from "**Anna Maria**" (see below), but little detail is available. "**Penpoll**" was apparently another small operation further up the Bosaneth valley on the eponymous farm, but likewise no detail has emerged. The mill at Trenarth bridge was purely a grist mill, but with three other mills in the Bosaneth valley, it is possible that there was mining apparatus present.

"Anna Maria mine". Named after Mrs Anna Maria Pender of Budock Vean, this was larger, and at the head of the creek (24) and 25). It was mainly a copper lode , first worked 1833 to 1835, It yielded 119 tons of copper ore valued at £792, but suffered from water ingress. The adventurers argued with each other, and the mine was shut and offered for sale. It was re opened in 1860 until about 1899, and was reported to have a good yield of copper, and small quantities of silver, and smaller still gold. It was reopened a third time in 1907, but pumping of 3000 gallons per minute was necessary to avoid flooding. Accounts made it obvious that water ingress made it uneconomic, and It closed finally about 1908. There was an unrelated Anna Maria mine in Devon, which confuses share values and yields in mining reports in the newspaper archives.

 There were also processing plants above Ponjeravah bridge (previous page), and at Polwheveral– where the blowing house is now a residential cottage (Lower Goongillings, on the left, after the bridge). This was on Scott land, for the output of **Wheal Caroline**, a small tin lode worked for ten years from 1850, and it is probable that the blow house was converted from a pre existing cottage. It was named after the daughter of Charles Scott, owner of Trewardreva and Goongillings, who also built the first Scott's quay in about 1820. The mine was a commercial failure.

References:

1. "Camborne School of Mines". *University of Exeter. Retrieved 19 May 2013*
2. Diodorus Siculus, volume 2 Library of History
3. The St Mawes Ingot, Baigree 1983
4. Mining in Devon and Cornwall, Wikipedia
5. The Early British Tin Industry, Tempus, Gerrard S : 2000
6. Records of Mining and Metallurgy, Phillips, J A and Darlington, J. London, 1857
7.The Metalliferous Mining Region of South-West England (Volume 1) Dines, H. G. 1956
8. Grace's Guide to British industrial History

Further reading:

Cornwall's Mining, Peter Stanier, Twelve heads press 1988

The Cornish mining Industry, a brief history. Buckley J.A., Tor Press 1992

8. Fishing and Oyster Farming

In the two decades after the second world war, Port Navas was widely known as the "Oyster village". It was said that one in three oysters consumed in Britain came from our Oyster Farm. In 2016 it remains the only commercial activity in the village. Shell middens have been used by archaeologists to identify ancient human presence around the globe, but it is surprising to learn from recent bone analysis at Bradford University[1], that in prehistoric Britain, sea food was rejected by the Pretannic people. (chapter three). What appears to be an irrational dietary fad was only changed when the Romans arrived. The native Oyster became a revered dietary treat, allegedly transported to Rome for festivals there[2]. The Romans introduced farmed beds throughout Britain, notably on the East and South coasts, but also in Swansea bay, and almost certainly Cornwall. However, the sometimes named "Roman oyster" Ostrea Edulis, is actually a native mollusc of our shores. Over the centuries, the social place of oysters has fluctuated from delicacy for the wealthy, to staple for the poor. Currently it could be described as a luxury to a minority, and not in the mainstream of favourite foods.

Oysters can be dredged in the wild, and also harvested from the foreshore at low tide. The principles of cultivation, handed down by the Romans, is:
1. Create rearing beds, by placing empty healthy shells ("Cultch") with parent oysters on the bed to allow a protected environment. Spat are then placed in growing areas to allow maturation.
2.Dredge the beds and examine the results, destroying any diseased oysters, muscles, sting winkle or star fish.
3.Avoid fishing during the spawning season May to October
4. Avoid overfishing.
Such was the dietary and financial importance of oysters that there is much documented legislation from medieval days. Dredging in the Thames was restricted in Elizabethan time between Easter and Lammas (wheat harvest festival). In 1638, Essex oyster production was restricted to 1000 barrels per week, and exports confined to the Prince of Orange and the Queen of Bohemia[3]. Dredging when there was no "R" in the month was a felony. Land owners with shoreline guarded their oysters jealously. Dr William Boxer Mayne fortunately documented records from the Merthen estate, the originals of which were lost in WW2.

In 1506, a Merthen document reads:
"From time before the memory of man, the Lorde of the Manor shall have the chief or best fish of all porpoises, thornpoles, dolphins and other great fish in the passage between Calamansack and Gweek". (A thornpole is a "magical beast like a blenny" - dogfish? Hard to imagine many Porpoises or Dolphins up the river!).

A manorial survey of 1580 refers to Oyster fishing worth £2 10s per year (This represents about £300,000 in 2016 currency, depending on method of calculating.).

A Merthen lease specifically excluded the dredging and taking of oysters. A 1658 document stated "Anchorage dues from Maen Broathe to Gweek Bridge are the rights of Sir Richard Vyvyan", and this was acknowledged by three members of the Mayn family of Lower Calamansack. In a hearing at the Court of Chancery in 1659[4], Sir Richard complains :

"Fishermen living on the banks of the Helford River including John Mayn of Constantine had dredged for oysters, refused to give up head fish and anchored and unloaded boats without paying dues" John Mayn said that he had seen a man pull down the Maen Broathe rock in 1654 or 55.The Vyvyan side won.

This may have been the John Mayn who died with £200 debt in 1695 (Chapter 3). This action was all during the Cromwellian regime, and the Judge perhaps perceived that Commonwealth days were numbered.

In 1681, William Gwavas of Carlyon, who had rented Merthen Manor with Calamansac from the Vyvyans, granted a sub lease to the contemporary Jonathan Mayn at Lower Calamansac, including "one little piece of land in the Downs of Calamansack Wollas where the said Jon Mayn do spread his nets". The rent was 20 shillings annually, plus the 1000 largest and best oysters. The agreement clearly included fishing and oysterage. Unfortunately, the Vyvyans disputed Gwavas' rights, and the agreement was revoked in 1712.

By 1815, the Helford River fishing rights were divided into upper, (above Maen Broath), and lower. The upper was let to Charles Scott of Trewardreva (£300), and the lower river to Francis Pender of Budock Vean (£50). The latter was sublet to James Mayn of lower Calamansack and Ponsaverran. James died that same year. 14 years later, in 1829, the Merthen estate leased the upper oysterage to John Tyacke, (tenant farmer of Merthen), for £450 per annum, and the Tyackes ran the oysters for the next 77 years. Farmer Tyacke was then aged 59, and his son, also John, continued the business. The Tyacke's also took over the Mayn interest. This was a sizeable operation. The annual rent alone was £13, 350 in 2015 values, so clearly it had also to be profitable.

In 1882, Tyackes ordered a purpose built vessel from Porthleven, with a wet hold (sea water running between watertight bulkheads. She was named "Rob Roy", and made weekly trips to Plymouth. They also undertook local sales, and dispatch by train up country. A major additional trade was sending spat oysters for laying down in the East Coast fisheries ready for the enormous London market. "Rob Roy", is described in appendix A.

Being readily poached, and with considerable difficulty in policing such an extensive water area, the Tyackes guarded their oyster beds with some ferocity. The summer assizes case of 1839 is summarised in an intimidating Flysheet published in 1846, which was distributed widely in the neighbourhood as a deterrent (overleaf). The "ultra lenient" sentence of six weeks hard labour seems disproportionate. One wonders whether the judgement was biased by pressure from vested interests.

CAUTION
STEALING OYSTERS.

The following is a copy of the Sentence of **Mr. JUSTICE COLERIDGE,** *on John Carlyon, John Williams and John Dudley who were Indicted at the Summer Assize 1839, for Stealing Oysters from the Oysterage of Sir. RICHARD RAWLINSON VYVYAN, Bart. in the HELFORD RIVER then and now occupied by Mr. JOHN TYACKE.*

SENTENCE

You have all been **CONVICTED** on the clearest evidence of **STEALING OYSTERS** from an **OYSTER BED, WELL MARKED OUT AND KNOWN.** There is a disposition on the part of the Prosecutor to deal leniently with you, and **I** am disposed to do the same, as all of you have received from the papers lying before me a very good and unexceptionable Character, and I believe all that is said in your favor. I am willing to hope **THAT WHAT YOU DID WAS UNDER A WRONG IMPRESSION,** though it would make you guilty in the eye of the law of **STEALING AND OF BEING CONSIDERED THIEVES.** I am very sorry that persons of your situation and character should have ever been brought into that position. It is always a reflection and a discredit where men of your character are brought up and placed at the prisoner's bar; it is indeed a great disgrace. **PROPERTY of THIS KIND** must be **PROTECTED.** It must be understood that **THE OWNER OF A FISHERY MUST BE AS SAFE IN THE ENJOYMENT AND POSSESSION OF HIS PROPERTY AS THE OWNER OF A HOUSE.** He has just as much right to it, He is paying a Rent of £450, a year for the enjoyment of it. *How is he to pay that Rent if all the people are to go and take away his Oysters, and if one can do it others may do it. YOU HAVE NO MORE RIGHT TO DO IT THAN YOU HAVE TO GO INTO A FIELD AND TAKE A SHEEP, therefore the thing must not be done again, or I shall certainly, if I should ever be here again and you are brought before me, treat you in a very different manner to that in which you will now be treated.* The only circumstance that interposes here between your having a very light punishment and a nominal punishment is, that you go in the night time in a considerable number, and that those with you have sticks, and that when the owners go there to protect their property, you turn upon one of the party and beat him with your sticks. If that is repeated it will be necessary to visit it with very severe punishment indeed. It would be like **a case of violent robbery which must be prevented** and if ever that force is repeated it will be treated most severely. What I am now going to do I hope will not be misunderstood. You appear to be three respectable young men who may have acted upon a mistaken notion, and therefore I am not only going to pass a light sentence, but I have been speaking to the gaoler who will take care that you are not placed along with low society to have your morals corrupted. The sentence of the Court is, and I hope its mildness will have a proper effect upon you, that you be imprisoned in the House of Correction for the space of six weeks, and that during that time you be kept to hard labour.

26). Widely posted warning notice by Grills and Hill regarding the criminal offence and likely penalty for nicking an oyster. It reports a case where "leniency" resulted in a mere prison sentence, rather than deportation!

In summarising, Judge Coleridge declared "Let it be a warning to others, that stealing oysters is no different from stealing sheep". Crikey! For the latter offence my great great uncle was deported to Australia, and lucky not to be hanged!

In 1847, a group of fishermen attempted to assert their right to fish and dredge in the river on the basis it was a public place[5]. John Tyacke (the younger) had coerced an armed naval cutter to confront the fishermen, but the captain declined to become involved, saying his remit was only to contain violence. Tyacke then moored a string of boats across the river from Calamansack to Maen Broathe, and hired a squad of local miners armed with bludgeons to keep the local men away. Vigilantes! So perhaps the Naval Cutter could justify action under these changed circumstance! But in view of the enormous rent charged, it was an important principle. By this time, Pond House in Polwheveral creek had been built as the depot for the oyster fishery, and remained so for 50 years. Another report concerned the 500ton Italian barque "Octavia Stella", grounding over the beds. The pilot incurred a £100 compensation order. In the 1890's, William Hodges, was appointed as Oyster Foreman and Bailiff . He had been trading with oysters in the Fal for 20 years and was the son of a bricklayer from Milton in Kent. He lived at Calamansack and was the first of four generations of that family engaged in the local trade (see below).

John Tyacke died in 1899, and his widow Elizabeth continued to run the estate. She is still recorded as running the oyster fishery in 1906 Kelly's, but she had probably died by then!

By now, the lower quay at Port Navas was available, and became the centre of operations.

In 1910, a syndicate called the "Original Helford Oysterage and Fishing Company" leased the lower fishery from Penryn Forryn, part of the Diocese of Exeter. They formed a registered limited company[6]. William Hodges was by now in an old age home at Budock, but his son Sydney continued in the trade, and may have been part of the syndicate. They sold in August 1915 to the Duchy of Cornwall for £1500. 4 months later, Sir Vyell Vivyan sold his rights of the upper river to the Duchy for £4,000, and the Duchy have remained owners to this day. In 1921, the tenancy was sold to Macfisheries, a wet fish retail chain created by the Lever brothers.in 1919. Sydney Hodges senior became manager on behalf of Macfisheries.

From the 1930's until the early 1980's, the oyster fishery was served by four vessels, three of which, originally Porthleven rowing seine boats, were very old work horses. **"Duchy"** was the oldest, built in 1828. 35 ft long, her working life extended to over 150 years. Sadly, on retirement in 1985 she was broken up . The other two, **"Glider"** and **"Helford"** were built in the mid 19th century.
An Essex built 40ft cockling boat, **"Reliance"** made trips to collect oysters from the Fal. One trip, she towed **"Birowlie"** (82) home with the pram(79) on her foredeck.

The Duke of Cornwall (later Edward V111) visited his Oyster farm on two occasions the current Duke (below). After 1948, much investment was made in the oyster farm by Macfisheries.

The third generation of Hodges, Sidney's son Leonard, took over as manager in 1952. Marketing and advertising raised awareness of the quality of Helford oysters. The sea tang and rich fleshiness is distinctive and arguably superior to others.

This seems to have been appreciated by royalty, because Prince Charles has visited on a number of occasions. The first time was in 1957, when the Royal Yacht anchored in mist off the river Mouth, and the Queen and Royal family came ashore by Royal barge. The river pilot, Howard Rendle, brought them up to Scott's quay, which had been specially dredged in advance. Prince Charles and the Duke of Edinburgh visited the Oyster farm, before re-joining the rest of the party. Because of the haze, nobody knew about the distinguished visitors, who also enjoyed a sunny picnic ashore by courtesy of a break in the clouds.

27). *Prince of Wales visits to the oyster farm. . Top left and right, and bottom left: May 21st, 1921. A large reception crowd gathered, with coaches from Falmouth. Accompanying is the Duke on the quay is Sir William Austin Bt . He was bailiff to the Duchy and lived at Trewince.*

28). *Bottom right, a second visit in 1937 was less formal.*

29). Left: Old Oyster farm about 1934. In the centre background shored up, is the hulk of a retired St Ives pilchard lugger, used as a shelter against easterly winds.

30). Right: Clearly no R in the month-the oyster boats are receiving annual maintenance—extra shed on the farm dates this to about 1945. The boats appear to have no engines yet (pre 1947). now less bulwarks. "Duchy " gets a lick of paint on her foredeck, whilst "Glider" has been inverted for some caulking .

Leonard Hodges took over the lease of the fishery when Macfisheries ceased trading in 1980 and he redeployed the title "Original Helford Oysterage and Fish company" for his new acquisition, as in the syndicate of which his Grandfather was a partner in 1910. When Leonard retired in 1997, his son Lindsey continued for a while as the fourth generation, but the business had challenges.

Bonamia oestreae - is a parasitic micro organism to which the oyster is particularly vulnerable. A major epidemic arose in the 1980's, and it has recurred since. It is possible that imported Gigas spat have caused spread of infection.

Meanwhile, in 2002, Ben Wright, a corporate lawyer from London and his brother in law Robin, a sound engineer and producer in the music industry, formed a partnership "Wright Brothers wholesale" delivering French oysters to London restaurants. In 2005 they acquired the Oyster Farm . This is an ambitious and challenging venture, which includes increasing the public appreciation of the mollusc—history repeating itself as when the Romans came to our shores. Apart from the labour and investment required in cultivating oysters, significant challenges remain. Bonamia re visited in 2011. In 2015, erroneous river water sampling suggested a problem with salmonella, which *protem* closed the fishery. Eventually this was shown to be a sampling error, but these things are sent to try.

31). Above left Working the dredge aboard "Glider". 32). Above right "Duchy" was the oldest of three working boats used by the farm for dredging and sorting. Built Porthleven, 1828 as a rowing Seine boat, 35ft long—a heavy boat to row. Acquired in 1934, they were fitted with engines by Skip Thomas in 1947., and remained in service until 1985. Henry Warren standing at the bow, Tiny Warren sitting. Ladies unknown.

33). Walking the days harvest up the beach to the processing plant, where it will be cleaned and sterilised before packing in kegs for dispatch.

34). Oyster farm about 1950. Loading a consignment for the train to London. The Morris light truck belonged to Fred Thomas. Restored, it made a triumphal return visit to the village in 2008. Arthur Rendle is rolling a keg onto the truck bed. Henry Warren to his left.

It would be incomplete to leave unmentioned the lobby group who don't want the lower quay used exclusively for commercial puposes. It is of course why it was built in the first place, but times, and the character of the location have moved on. A conservation sentiment exists to protect the quay.

However the village needs wage earning permanent residents, and most people will wish this contemporary project every success. It is an industry steeped in the villages history, and a tangible raison d'etre . Knibb's engineering at Trenarth, and Henry Collins at Inow Farm are the only other local businesses.

References:
1. Archaeology: Sharp shift in diet at onset of Neolithic. Michael p Richard. Nature 2003
2. Oyster. Rebecca Stott 2004
3. Essex Victoria County History 1994: Colchester Oyster fishery
4. Chancery Records, 1659. NRO
5. Royal Cornwall Gazette 02.04.1847
6. Records of the Duchy of Cornwall

9. Granite, Iron Ore, Coal, Timber, Guano and Lime - life in the evolving village in the 19th and early 20th century.

In the latter half of the 19th century, the country was engaged in a frenzy of property development, and Port Navas was caught in the tide. Both the Granite and mining industries increased the need for manpower, and extra accommodation was required. The commercial boom years were the 1860's and 70's. In 1870, Brogden's mine was in full production, delivering 2000 tons of ore, and Freeman's shipped 3657 tons of granite the following year, needing probably well over 100 ships annually for both commodities.

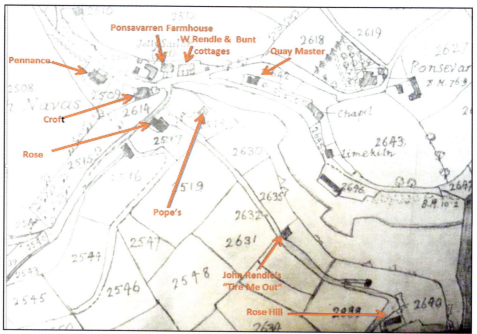

35). 1878 Ordnance Surveymap. Pub has received extension. Third terrace at creek head not yet built. Location of "Pope's" and "Tire Me Out". Old Ponsavarren ground plan, and old top road. Rose hill was then called Cheiloo cottage, reflecting the old name of the upper creek (see appendix C)

Even in 1891, Lane described it as "This busy little Port" (chapter 9).

The Maynes of Ponsaverran were inveterate developers, and the impetus to build a second quay arose soon after Freemans took the lease in 1856. Whereas the first quay road could be mainly backfilled from the adjacent hill behind the abutting wall, the extended road to the lower quay required extra material to be brought in. An easy supply of shale and slate was available from the cliff adjacent to the Constantine road above Croft Cottage. This became a quarry for such material, and appears to have been exploited for the extended quay road project, as well as for other village work. After completion of the quay, this quarry site, which was on Trefusis land, became a potential housing plot, and is where Pennance (1870's) was built. A further source of material came from a quarry opposite the new lower quay, on Budock Vean land. William Mayne died in 1863, soon after the project was completed. Josiah, "Captain" Joe" Mayne, replaced his older brother at Ponsaverran, and undertook further developments. to improve amenities for the community, The stream was trained with a revetting wall running from above Trewince lane to the creek head. This possibly included a rebuilt bridge at Trewince Lane. The ford was abolished by diverting the stream to cross the road more perpendicular, and constructing a low bridge (the tunnel under the road which is occasionally overwhelmed by heavy rain, recreating the "ford effect". The stream thus moved to the Calamansack side of its original course, and the pub, modernised and extended, incorporated some reclaimed ground.

In about 1895, a semi detached pair of houses were built adjacent to the coal storecalled Shearwater and Firleigh (the latter probably named after a hamlet near the Rev James Mayne's old Parish in Devon). His son Ambrose was likely advising his ageing father.

Ambrose had a close friendship with the Seager family, to the extent that he allegedly had "Trewince House" built for them, on the upper fields of the eponymous farm, which had been bought from the Boadens (see chapter 4). In the event, the Seagers moved into Ponsaverran and became Ambrose Mayne's surrogate family . The new Trewince House was used as a rest home initially, then leased, to C.T. Hammerton Esq from Yorkshire. He was evidently a man of substance, and hired Captain Peter Pascoe from Porthleven as skipper for his yacht on the river (see below). During WW1, a Captain Denton also lived there. He later married a sister of the Rev James Mayne's second wife. In 1920, Trewince became the residence of Sir William Austin, Bailiff to the Duchy (see chapter 8). He also came from Yorkshire.

Ambrose Mayne instigated a new village hall, on ground regained by Captain Joe's stream project. This had a men's reading room, and wash room for the ladies . (I know, but it was the culture of then!). At the same time, a clean water supply was introduced, by creating a small stream diversion on the common ground opposite Pennance. This passed through a housed filter bed (still there), which was connected via a pipe, laid down the stream to a stand pipe on the wall outside the new village hall (tap still partially there). On the Ponsaverran side of the filter bed, an overshoot waterwheel and pump house provided filtered water to Ponsaverran. All this work was completed in 1903.

The Trefusis estate built a new dwelling on a pre existing site towards Calamansack above Croft Cottage (now Rose Cottage). This was rented by John Tremayne, farmer and horse dealer.

63

A small cottage on Trefusis land was possibly partially demolished to make space for the new training wall, and finally levelled when the village hall was built. It shows on the 1842 tithe map, and the 1878 Ordnance Survey. The Rendle children of the 1930's remember the ruins. This small "hovel" became known as Pope's Cottage, which name survives for the small public garden beside the village hall. The only Pope ever living in the village was a 12 year old orphan, Thomas, at Inow Cottages, and seems unlikely to be connected. Likewise, papal religious associations are improbable in a Wesleyan Protestant and Church of England community. Pope is however a common surname in Cornwall with strong local representation. A Falmouth shipping firm was run by Edwin Pope of Arwenack House. The company were both ship owners and merchants, originating from Boscastle, and had a fleet of fruit ships to Spain and the Canaries. Many such vessels also engaged in the granite trade using Port Navas quay. One was "Queen of the Chase", 98 tons, built for Pope's by James Mayn, (a Falmouth shipbuilder not directly related to Port Navas Maynes. (see chapter 9 and appendix A). It may be that firm used this empty cottage as an office, in the same way Freeman's used Mayn Cottage. The Seaman's chapel (Mayn Cottage) was still functioning, but one end was taken over by Freeman's as an office.

By 1881, the census recorder suggests the village was no longer referred to as "Cove", and it was forming a clearer identity. The population had risen to 64, of which 19 were children, described as "scholars". The nearest school, opened in 1836, was at Ponjaravah - quite a walk. The iron miners from the 1870's had gone, but there were many stone masons, and also several road workers.

At the time of this census, the pub was closed, probably coincident with the large extended front (as above) which was built in the 1870's. This seems to have capitalised on reclaimed ground after culverting and training the stream. The pub had traded since soon after the quay opened in 1831, as a double fronted building facing the stream (chapter 4). Originally it was called "the Sailor", later becoming "Jolly Sailor". It had a succession of landlords from the village, few of whom stayed long. The road to Constantine crossed the stream by ford at the lowest point, some yards below the present bridge under the road (built in the late 1870's). The stream ran past the front of the pub, which would certainly have simplified the task of sobering up unruly customers. Re-opened after the rebuild by 1891, reports suggest it may have become overly "Jolly", with drunkenness and fights, particularly after the annual Good Friday cockling tradition, held on Calamansack bar. Miners from Constantine and local mariners converged, leading to fights, and chaos. It seems the Rev James Mayne closed it down, and it remained shut for a while. Later it was reopened by widowed Elizabeth Ann Rendle (p 66) as a guest house, and then the "Temperance Hotel" - oh dear, no beer!

Thus for nearly 120 years, the environment had the stream of heavy waggons transporting granite and iron ore to the quays, plus considerable building and construction activity. Busy and noisy. What would residents say today?

The 1911 census provides a snapshot of the community then, including families whose descendants are well within living memory.

Lower Calamansack population by then was down to 15 in three households, all farming except for one fisherman. Higher Calamansack had 4 residents, and the head is a farmer. Inow has 13 with two farmers, Treworval has 13 and two farmers, as does Drift and Treviades. Trenarth has two farmers and 7, - making a total of 65 in the out lying farms. In the village proper, there are 19 residences with a total population of 88. Of the wage earners, there is 1 builder, 1 carpenter,1 granite cutter, 2 mariners, 2 oyster fishermen, and 7 involved in agriculture. The activities at the quay do not seem to have offered significant employment other than the oyster farm at lower quay. Graham Rogers building and yacht repair business later changed this.

Some names from this census stand out. The Warren family were living in a cottage at Trenarth Bridge (36.). This house had 6 rooms. Head of the house is John Stamford Warren, (1869-1972). He was a farm labourer born in Plymouth. A small man, but he and his wife Emily, had no less

36). Cottage at Trenarth Bridge

than 8 children, most of whom were noticeably oversize. They became iconic figures in Port Navas into the 1970's. Nellie was the oldest daughter and remained a spinster, living with her bachelor brother William ("Tiny"). We don't know how many offers of betrothal the pair may have turned down. "Tiny" was a gentle but huge man, who worked on the oysters. Henry, his immediate younger sibling did likewise, but when he married, moved into the middle of the row of creek head cottages, previously occupied by Captains Bate and Bunt. The youngest sibling, Walter became a stone mason and builder. (see chapter 12 for post war Warrens).

Albert Rendle, who had been mate on his father William's Ketch "Howard" when she shipped the last load of granite for Tower Bridge from Port Navas in 1894, was living with his wife and six children in the first creek head house which his family had leased since the 1850's (now called "the Cottage"). Originally this was a detached double fronted dwelling, before the terraces were added. The Rendle family were all mariners, originally from Plymouth, as follows:
John Rendle (1805), mariner, had two sons, John (1833) and William (1835), who also went to sea in the coastal trade. In 1851, aged 28 and 26, the brothers were skipper and mate of the schooner **"Delabole"**. They made frequent calls to Port Navas, no doubt carrying Constantine granite for the new steam dock project. In Port Navas, they both found local girls. John married Sarah Hocking, the daughter

of a Port Navas barge man. They lived in a cottage which was on the site of Dinyan's garage. It was called "Tire Me Out" - allegedly because John Rendle found too many children tedious. Brother William married Mary Jane Tremayne, a farmer's daughter from Inow. They lived in the double fronted creek head cottage. (Now "The Cottage"). William and Mary Jane had a first born son in 1858, also called William, who in turn, like his forebears and other male siblings, went to sea. He married Elizabeth Ann Humphrey of Port Navas. In 1898, he was drowned, leaving Elizabeth Ann a widow, with two sons and a daughter all under five. The bereaved family moved into the closed pub together with Elizabeth's spinster sister, and ran it as a guest house. Later in his seafaring career William senior was rendered blind when his ship was struck by lightning off the Runnelstone. He died aged seventy in 1905.

37). c. 1905, the village hall just opened. Poor horse grinding up to Ponsaverran. Manure at Blamey's. A pitched roof shed is seen between Plumtree and Shearwater. Winn's coal store and Smithy far right.

38). Around 1910 and busy! Three empty carts either collecting manure or coal. Believed to be Dr Blamey's car (unrelated to the grain merchant) is parked outside the village hall. The maids in uniform are most likely from the Temperance hotel, as in 54). Behind the hall, there is now a privy for Gents and Ladies—c.f. 37). Mrs Pankhurst's influence?

39). Above: Tinted card, also about 1910. Quay gate house clearly seen. Blamey's sign over the manure store door. Uncertain what the posts are doing alongside, as in 38). Wrong colour for Plumtree!

40). About 1920. Manure store roof looks new. Note the blacksmith's shop beside Firleigh

41.) Estate map of Ponsaverran 1926, showing new and current road (pink) and old road (green).

Tragedy struck the village in 1883 as follows. John Ould was a widower fisherman who had lived in Croft Cottage for many years. In 1868 His daughter Annie married Phillip Colwill, a mariner from Clovelly. In 1871, Annie and her one year old daughter were living with her father at Croft Cottage. It was common for sailors wives to live with their parents, but Annie latterly also had to look after her frail father. There were signs of strain in the marriage. It seems likely that her father negotiated with the Trefusis estate managers to build a house on the roadside quarry next door, possibly with his daughter and son in law in mind. The new house (later named "Pennance" by Graham Rogers, below) was complete in the 1878 ordinance map, and in 1881, the entry for the new house records the Colwill family. By now there were two children—Edith 11 and her younger brother Philip age 5. The Colwill's appear to have been the first tenants, and in the area, leases covered three generations. Allegedly, father Philip drank heavily when ashore, and left the family without support. In 1883, a desperate Annie left her children with her brother at Trenarth Bridge, saying she was going shopping in Falmouth. In fact she returned to Pennance and hanged herself from a beam in an out building. The children were fostered by others in the village, young Philip living with farmer Rail at Calamansack. Edith eventually moved up country and married. Sailor father Philip died of chronic meningitis (usually tuberculous) in 1888. Young Philip had title to the lease on Pennance, but turned his back on it and joined the metropolitan police. According to his son, who visited some years ago from Canada, Philip could not bear to return to Port Navas. The house remained empty for some while, and a big cloud hung over the village.

By 1891, a family called Exelby had rented the place, and the stigma gradually dwindled. A daughter Elizabeth ("Zoe") married Captain Tom Collings .(chapter 11). By 1901, Richard Thomas and family had moved into the house from Treglidwith farm. He had been a stone mason in the granite quarries, but died that year, leaving a wife, Elizabeth, and two daughters Ellen and Minnie. Ellen ran a tobacconist and confectionary business from a back room of the house, and Minnie was a dress maker, and this paid the rent. Then in 1907, the adventurers re-opening Anna Maria mine engaged a young carpenter, AG Graham Rogers, from a successful family of Falmouth builders. He built new engine house (see chapter 7). Graham's friends advised him that he should get married, and that there were nice young ladies in the house in which the Colwill tragedy had occurred. A year later he married Ellen ("Helena"). Minnie and her mother moved out. The house was called Pennance after the Rogers family home near Pennance Point at Swanpool. By 1911, Graham was described as a self employed builder. He joined the Royal Flying Corps for the hostilities, and in 1919 he and Helena bought the freehold of Pennance from Lord Trefusis. They had already developed the place into a thriving refreshment room, providing teas for tripper boat passengers from Falmouth. These used the lower quay to disembark when tides permitted (43, 44)). Advanced phone calls from Prince of Wales Pier told Mrs Rogers how many to expect, and the business clearly blossomed. Graham also took over a workshop on the upper quay coining the name "Yacht Yard",

68

42). Thought to be blind Captain William Rendle washing clothes in the stream, soon after the course had been diverted and bridged. From Trewince Lane, the stream wall is constructed in local slate, vertically laid, with no mortar. It directs the water south of its original route, towards the road. Back fill has generated the ground on which Chestnut cottage stands. The road bridge is a substantial structure easily overlooked, and must have caused mayhem to traffic when it was being made . It comprises two walls of 12" by 12" by 24" granite blocks, continuing the course of the diverted stream. The channel provided is 5 ft. wide. The walls are spanned by 12" by 12" by 7ft 6"granite slabs laid parallel. There is no sign of subsidence. Where the small tributary from the Calamansack hill joins the main stream, a washing pool with steps down was created, probably when the village hall was built, (all this still there to be seen). Captain Rendle is using this washing facility. Date uncertain, but he died in 1905. "Rose Cottage", then residence of one branch of the horse dealing Tremaynes is in the background, with Mrs Tremayne and her daughter outside their porch (could be Euphemia).

and developed a boat repair business in addition to his building work. The couple were thus in the vanguard of Port Navas tourism. Later, Messrs Bate, Moyle and Tremayne also offered teas.

In the first two decades of the 20th century, the quay road had a gate onto the main road to exclude public passage, perhaps to prevent pilfering. Whilst granite was too heavy to steal, the further commercial venture which had begun in the 1890's was easier. ML Blamey and Son were agricultural merchants, and farmers from Veryan. They had developed a large business network over 30 years, selling seed, and fertiliser products. They also ran the auctions at Truro market. Thomas Blamey, son of the founder, built a store immediately after the new Port Navas quay gate, for fertiliser, and occasionally grain. Some stock was kept in the open, behind posts alongside the quay road. Blameys advertised supplies from there between 1897 and 1923. The shed was known as the Manure Store (now "Bosoljack", at the time of writing, it is for sale as a desirable waterside residence). The manure was mainly guano from Iquique in Southern Chile, brought to England by the last fleet of Cape Horn square riggers. By 1899, Freeman's had pulled out, and confined their granite business to Penryn. With the departure of Freeman's and the shrinkage of the granite trade, the lease was available again. Demand for coal remained considerable. There were steam engines on farms, mines and quarries, as well as domestic consumption for the popular Cornish ranges. Many vessels were delivering coal to the quay in the latter part of the 19th century, handled by Captain William Bunt (Chapter 13). This commodity could also have attracted unwanted attention from the light fingered.

The resident houses on the quay road 1n 1900 were the quay masters house, built by the Freemans in 1870, Shearwater, Firleigh, and "Mayn Cottage", (converted in 1904 into a double dwelling from the old Freeman's office and Chapel). The first tenant of Shearwater was Edwin Williams, described in 1901 as a coal merchant. Between the new semidetached houses and Mayn Cottage was a coal store (now the site of the residence called "the Garage"). In 1902, Winn's, an established Penryn coal merchant, took a lease on the quays. 15 year old John Constantine Winn (1887-1978), son of a Constantine farmer and nephew of the owner of the coal firm, became the coal quay manager for them in 1905. This would almost certainly have included a takeover of Edwin William's business by the Penryn firm. By 1911, Edwin, still in Shearwater, was foreman of the oyster fishery. The Winn enterprise secured a continuing use for the quays, which were the heart of the new village. Early years were sufficiently successful that later (1925) he was able to purchase the freehold of the quay and quay road. This business continued throughout the 1930s. In order to allow easier unloading at lower states of tide, a half tide quay was built to the south of the lower quay of 1860. Proceeding past the fragrance of guano, the smell of Welsh coal would enter the nostrils, and perhaps coal smoke from the lime kiln.

First tenant at Firleigh was John Moyle, a tin miner from Wendron. He had a wife Elizabeth, daughter Ellen and son John Arthur ("Toby"). He died in 1908, possibly of lung disease, leaving Elizabeth a widow. By 1911, Ellen had moved away, and Toby was a carpenters apprentice. In 1915, Toby married Harriet Symonds, one of eight children of a granite mason from Ponjaravah, and his mother moved to Helston where Ellen had settled. This left the newly weds with the tenancy at Firleigh. In 1924, when Blamey and Sons ceased trading from Port Navas, Toby Moyle took over the manure store as his workshop. A John Moyle from Constantine who did voluntary construction work on the new chapel (chapter 10), seems unrelated.

Fred and Bunny Thomas were newly married when they visited Port Navas in 1926 and determined to settle here. Fred grew up in Bexley Heath, and had served an apprenticeship with Fraser and Chalmers of Erith At the time of his marriage he was working for Powell Duffryn of Aberdare— then the worlds biggest coal mining company. He was engineer in charge of installing the winding gear for the Ocean Deep Colliery, Treharris, Glamorgan. (Now diversified, this firm remains a multi million pound organisation). They bought Firleigh from Ambrose Mayne , and the coal store from John Winn, shortly before Winns sold the wharfage to Annear's. Fred was a typical engineer, highly inventive, perfectionist and contemptuous of workmanship below his exacting standard. He was much respected by all who knew him. He built a garage on the coal store site, and the coal store had to be re located on the creek head, removing the second privy from the village hall, in what is now Mrs Lucas's garden. Toby and Harriet Moyle apparently were not aware of the new ownership, and suddenly needed a roof over their heads. With help from other villagers, he built one level accommodation on top of the old manure store, and the young couple moved in after nine months. It was never quite finished. A doorway at the

43). Steamer SS "Queen of the Fal 2" with passengers waiting to re embark on a return trip in the 1930s. Owned by River Fal Steamship Co, she was a regular caller. The passengers could buy teas at Mrs Moyle (Bosoljack), Mrs Tremayne (Croft), Bate's (Old Jolly Sailor), and Mrs Rogers (Pennance). The trips began in 1907, and continued until WW2. (see appendix). Notice three granite blocks on the quay, and a shed. Only one block there now, and in a different position. Who nicked the other two? This vessel also acted as tug, towing Port Navas schooners in and out of port. Could that be the same pram dinghy in the foreground as the post war image page 91?

44). Around 50 passengers heading for tea. The date, 1926, is certain because Mr and Mrs Moyle's house over the Manure store is under construction..

Evolving Upper Quay, 1875 to late 1930's

45). Left 1875. Scotch Derrick, showing steps on the Samson post, for servicing the gear. Assuming 12" steps, this makes the post 32 ft. high. The jib is facing away, and is dropped approximately 45 degrees, with the elevating cable roughly horizontal. By Pythagoras, the jib is approximately 45ft. Hard to lift a block weighing 2 tons 50 ft., so perhaps Lane in his guide of 1891 was exaggerating. The Scotch Derrick jib reached the stone deposited by the travelling crane, and delivered it either to the finishing shed, or to the hold of the ship direct.

46). Above, 2016. granite slab with cast iron insert was the swivel base for the Scotch Derrick Samson post, still present on the upper quay, , it is all that remains.

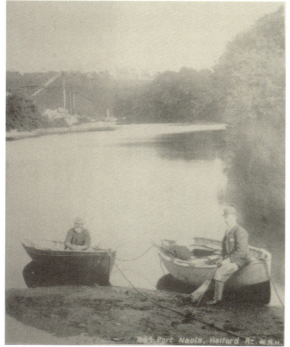

47). Left. Estimated 1910, with Captain Charles Rendle and John Seager (in plus fours) looking philosophical at the creek head, quay in the background. Stacks of granite blocks dropped from the gantry, and coal to the right. On the western corner of the quay is a vertical post mounted on a granite slab. Looking like a menhir, it was perhaps an anchor for swinging blocks from the gantry. Lift and manoeuvring were achieved by hand winches. The blocks of granite are at least a cubic yard, and would have weighed 2 1/2 tons. Imagine carriage on a horse waggon. Clearly shipment was still undertaken at this time. (Hawke)

48). 1920's. The "Menhir" is still on the west corner of the quay, but the blocks have gone.

49). Date uncertain, but likely 1920s. Boat and 5 children are Rendles. Scotch Derrick shows on upper quay, Mayne cottage to the left. Seine nets in foreshore (Hawke)

50). Creek 1930. The spoil from Skip Thomas's fuel tank excavation (right) is still fresh.

51). Upper quay late 1930s. Motor coaster possibly the MV "Regina". Notice at left, piles of coal and chalk or road stone stored in front of the steel gantry frame, away from discharge wharf. Lime was stored in steel containers in enclosure at right end of quay. The Scotch derrick is demolished. (Hawke)

front for an intended balcony, which never materialised. Guests would have had a big surprise opening this door by mistake. He and Harriet remained there for the rest of their days, and were notable characters in the village. Shearwater was occupied in 1938 by a Mr and Mrs Gough, and the house became a polling booth for the local election that year. They also offered teas to visiting tripper boats.

The Thomas's neighbour on the other side, in the old Seaman's chapel, was retired Captain Tom Collings. (see above and chapter 11) He was master of "Guiding Star" during the first world war. Her winter lay up berth was in the creek, stern to Mayn Cottage. (appendix A) When Dr Blamey from Penryn (different family) was delayed attending another delivery, "Zoe" Collings acted as midwife at the birth of Sally Thomas (her mother's second confinement).

In the between wars period, Ambrose Mayne apparently found it necessary to sell off some of his estate. This included all properties on the quay road, "Trevean", and the upper quay. He retained the Lime kiln, which according to Kelly's was worked by Freeman, Sons and Co until WW2, but it may not be so. Shipments for Blamey's and Winn's became spasmodic in the 1930s. Richardson's at Gweek were a competing firm, and their operation was bigger. The abandoned **"Sunbeam",** whose keel remains opposite the upper quay (see appendix A) was a sailing grain barge. Beached in a leaking state just before World War 2, she had perhaps also carried materials for Blamey's . In the first half of the 20th century, vessels at the quay might have been discharging Chalk, Sand, Bricks, Guano or Coal. In order to retain stability, the ships had to have ballast in the hold after discharging. How did they ballast when granite was no longer shipped? Possibly they carried sufficient permanent ballast to remain seaworthy, which would have reduced space in the hold for cargo.

Next door to the Rendles at the creek head, the middle terraced cottage was occupied by a succession of seafarers. Captain Uden appears to be the first tenant, and was master of a 36 ton vessel in 1851. Captain Bunt then occupied it until he moved away, at which point, the brother of his son in law, Captain Steven Bate, became the occupant for over 50 years. He had married Euphemia, the daughter of farmer and horse trainer John Tremayne, who lived at Rose Cottage. Steven Bate had come ashore in 1879, initially working as a cowman for his wife's father. When Elizabeth Ann Rendle moved to Mawnan, he and Euphemia took over the old pub, officially now called the "Temperance Hotel", although the name never seemed to catch on. They did teas, hired boats, and offered accommodation(55, 56). Steven built an outshut onto the Temperance hotel which became a general store and post office, and he became post master. Later on, he also worked in the Oyster farm. Peter Pascoe and his wife moved from Trevean into the end terraced cottage, and the Bates moved into Trevean until 1928, when it was sold by Ambrose Mayne to a Miss Rashleigh. The "hotel" was leased to Macfisheries, and occupied as a home by the Hodges family, who renamed it Chestnut Cottage, but the shop and post office was taken over by Captain Tom Collings through the 1930s (chapter 11).

Captain Peter Pascoe, who had come to Port Navas as Mr Hammerton's yacht skipper (see above), remained in the village for the rest of his life. He moved from Trevean to the end creek head cottage, becoming neighbour to the Bates. Steven and Euphemia Bate moved into Trevean, until the house was sold to a Miss Rashliegh, when the Bates moved into the one bedroom middle terrace . This had, recently been vacated by Captain Bunt, who had moved to Mawnan . In 1931, aged 78, Peter told his wife that he was going to try for a bass. He had been seen in the afternoon by several people, but he never returned, and the body was found washed up some days later. Farmer White had the tenancy of Ponsaverran farm from the early 1930s until about 1952. He and his wife lived in the farmhouse (Now called "ChyanDowr") until after the war.

As local carpenter, Toby Moyle also acted as undertaker, hand making coffins when required. A story of drama surrounds the burial at sea of John Mortimer in 1933. He was a retired vicar from Warwickshire, and had "Elishir" built in the 1920's (later called "Inow House"). He had expressed a wish to be committed to the deep. Toby made the coffin, and Mr Mortimer's launch, the **"Gem"**, was used for the "service". The party comprised Captain Tom Collings, Skip Thomas, Toby Moyle and the Reverend Thomas Webber conducted the proceedings. The morning assigned brought brisk south westerly weather, with a good sea running off the Manacle buoy. Neither Toby Moyle nor Thomas Webber were robust sailors, and struggled with sea sickness. Following reading the committal, the coffin was slipped overboard, but, and despite what was believed to be ample additional weights, it refused to sink. Under Tom Collings chastisement, Toby produced an auger to let out air - a tough if unusual challenge of seamanship, the coffin crashing into "Gem" with each big sea, threatening to stove in her planking. It is a miracle they weren't maimed, let alone drowned, but in the end, the lord looked kindly on their efforts, the augers did their work, and the party returned to Port Navas.

Returning to Trewince., in 1921 the house was leased by Sir William Austin, Bt. He was the son of a wealthy Yorkshire landowner and MP, and came to Cornwall as Bailiff to the Duchy. He escorted the Duke in the Royal Visit of 1921. During the 1920s, both his daughters were married in Constantine, and Port Navas was bedecked with flags for the occasion, with a celebratory party arranged for the villagers. Trewince garden was a particular show piece. Sir William left for a sunny climate on Doctor's advice in 1930. A Capt Busk moved in in the 1930s, and in 1939 it sold as a Country guest house to a Mr and Mrs Gealer who ran it through the war years. At about the same time as the Thomas's and Moyle's were re - profiling the quay road, the Warington Smyths moved to Upper Calamansack. They were an illustrious family. Admiral William Smyth (1788-1865), was Chief Hydrographer to the Admiralty, and married Annarella Warington. Their son Warington Wilkinson Smyth FRS, was a 19th century mining engineer who became professor of the Royal School of Mines—part of Imperial College. He was mineral advisor to the Duchy, and

75

Had lived in Marazion for 30 years. A keen yachtsman, it is his Memorial Cup which is the trophy for the annual Falmouth to Fowey passage races. Knighted in 1888, he died in 1890, and his widow moved to St Erth, where they are both buried. Sir Warington had two sons, Nevil (who was awarded a VC at Khartoum in 1898) and Herbert, who followed his father into mining. Herbert also gained recognition as a traveller and writer. He served in the RNVR as Lieutenant Commander, and was mentioned in dispatches in WW1. He spent his later working life in South Africa where he was Secretary for Mines and Industries, and retired to Falmouth in 1927. He had three sons and a daughter- Bevil, Nigel, Rodney and Elizabeth. He bought Calamansack, and built a house there from re-cycled Boer war Barrack sheds. He was, like his father, a keen yachtsman, and two of his sons—Bevil and Nigel were very successful yacht and boat designers. After the war, Nigel and Bevil took over Falmouth Boat Construction.

It is appropriate at this point to mention the Port Navas efforts during the two world wars.

During the 1914-18 war, several men of the village served with the armed forces, and some never returned. As mentioned above, Graham Rogers served with the Royal Flying Corps. Some of the sailing commercial vessels became armed merchantmen, including Captain Collings with **" Guiding Star" (**Chapter 12)**.** Military training occurred locally. There were army stables in Trewince lane, converted in the 1960s into domestic accommodation by John Shuffrey . An army rifle range was also established on the Calamansack bank of Polwheverell creek, which continued to be used until after the second war.

In the 1939-45 conflict, Helford became the base for an extraordinary top secret activity, under the RN Special Operations Unit. This was conceived by, amongst others, Ian Lancaster Fleming, (of James Bond fame), who worked for the Naval Intelligence Division. One can see where some of his fantasy writing came from. The highly risky operation was engaged in the transfer of agents and escaped British servicemen from occupied Europe. The Special Service Unit Inshore Boat Squadron operated a fleet of vessels disguised as French Tunny men. It initially ran from Dartmouth and Falmouth but in 1940, became based on the Helford river. In depth knowledge of German habits in supervising the Breton fishing was obtained from escaped French fisherme. The vessels were painted for each mission to simulate part of the Breton fleet. After an overnight passage, they mingled with the fleet on the French side, mimed trawling for a few days so that the Germans would be convinced of their authenticity, and then the charge was transferred under cover of dark. The French resistance was crucial. This routine experienced no detection, right under the noses of the German Navy. Originally the flotilla was formed from actual French vessels, but later, high speed vessel capable of 25 knots were employed. One was called **"Angel Rouge".** She retained the profile of a French tunny boat above water but was of planing form below. To simulate a thumping single cylinder hot bulb engine,

76

52). Creek head, late October about 1922. The "Bate's Store" sign is still over the door at Chestnut, but no telegraph poles have yet appeared. The "swing arm" Morgan 2 seater AF 5929, was bought new by Alfred Hawke, the postcard photographer in 1914. He worked from 1905 until he died in 1977, producing nearly 40,000 images. An identical 1913 Morgan is in the Science Museum collection, London.

53). Pennance about 1930. The shed (without flagpole) survives on the other side of the road, as my studio. At the near corner of the garden retaining wall, a stone marks the Vivyan/Trefusis boundary. Stucco facing has now been removed to restore the original stone work. (Hawke)

54). Croft about 1925. Store in foreground and shelter up the hill are gone. The telegraph pole by Pennance is still there. Mrs Tremayne's chickens and "Tea" signboard are seen. Mrs Webber once hit a chicken driving her AC car, and duly replaced it. (Hawke).

55). Steven and Euphemia Bate outside "Bates", about 1918. Luncheon, teas, rooms and boats for hire. Plants for sale, Post office and shop completed. (Hawke)

56). With uniformed maid and unknown baby, early 1920s. Sign re painted "Fresh milk and cream daily" cf (55)above.

57). 1940. Captain Steven Bate, outside his cottage, with arthritic hips,

58). Tom Collings and his daughter in the 1930s outside the Post Office, which the family took over from the Bates.

59). Penjerrick's Thornycroft bus awaiting passengers outside the post office,?1936. Mrs Tremayne still doing teas. New telegraph pole since image of 1922. Rendle children outside Village Hall. Stand pipe is still the only water supply. (Hawke)

60). Villagers at Ponsavarren 1930. Back row Jack Rendle, Sid Harvey, Farmer Ould, Mrs Peters, Millie Tremayne Middle row Mrs White, ? Edith Tremayne
Front row, Johnny Vague, Capt Steven Bate, Capt Peter Pascoe (of Porthleven) came to Port Navas as yacht skipper to Mr Hammerton of Trewince. He drowned whilst fishing alone in 1931, age 78.

61). Albert and Eva Jane Rendle with their family outside the Cottage, about 1930.
Left to right, Howard, Marjorie, ?William, ?John, ?Herbert, Arthur and Gordon.

a crew member was deployed to generated smoke puffs through a false exhaust pipe. One day a fire broke out, and before it could be extinguished, a German patrol vessel came to offer assistance. They were assured . In best Franco German, that it was not required!

Lord Runciman's schooner "**Sunbeam 2"** was requisitioned as mother ship and accommodation vessel for other ranks.

62. Sub Lieutenant Howard Rendle DSC in uniform

63). Photograph and painting of HMS Sunbeam 2 moored on the river (Lord Methuen, R.A.)

64). Landing craft at Trebah, loading GI's for the Normandy landing, 1944.

81

Herbert Warington Smyth became resident CO of Helford until he died in 1941, Bevil Warington Smythe was in command of the Special Operations Executive, based at "Redifarne" above Bar beach, whilst his brother Nigel was senior officer, inshore patrol division (SIS). Nigel designed a special surf boat for going in on the Brittany beaches.

The Warington Smyth's needed competent dependable seamen with local knowledge and recruited Howard Rendle, son of Albert, who was serving with the navy in Scapa Flow at the time. He joined the Helford unit, and was involved in several dangerous missions. On 24th December 1943, he recovered 25 people from Ile Stagadon off L'Aberwrack, amongst escaped airmen was an agent who carried information of German V2 installations. Howard was awarded a DSC. He was made

65). Creek from Dinyan garden, 1930s. (Hawke) Foreground tree obscures Scotch derrick which is still there. Oyster House yet to be built. Flag pole outside Ponsaverran. The lime kiln appears derelict. The travelling crane is removed, but the iron frame rail is still present, as is the granite dressing shed and smithy's shop.

66). Early 1930s Hawke photograph (detail of 71). The travelling crane gantry is still present, as is base of the Scotch Derrick (obscured by bushes, resembles a tree trunk!).

67). Upper and lower quay 1930s. The oyster farm's "Helford" is moored off the quay. Identity of yacht unknown. The bank appears steeper than present. No sign of the shelter for "Queen of the Fal " passengers (Hawke).

68). 1930s. The converted ship's lifeboat which eventually disintegrated on opposite bank, belonged to Graham Rogers. Rendle flatty and Gordon Rendle's punt ever present. Skip Thomas's motor boat moored under the garage, and derrick still seen on the quay. New shed on quay side. (Hawke).

sub lieutenant. Howard's brother Arthur, and Skip Thomas serviced the fleet and machinery, commissioned by the war office. Graham Rogers was also heavily involved as a shipwright.

Between 1939 and 1945, Falmouth received considerable attention from German bomber and fighter raids. Men working on the concrete landing slip at Trebah beach were raked with machine gun fire by raiding Messerschmitts. This was preparation for the American contribution to operation Neptune. Landing craft from Trebah were part of the carnage at Utah (64).

A house opposite the quay on Budock Vean's side was destroyed by a direct hit from an incendiary bomb. The explosion stunned a lot of fish, which were easy pickings for the villagers suppers. Sally and Robin Thomas were taken by their father to witness the inferno in the dark, as a lesson on the destructiveness of war. The rebuilt house was eventually bought by a retired Swansea GP, Dr Seward. He had a 38ft yacht "Freckles" moored to half tide piles on the shore. He sailed her single handed to Spain at the age of 85. Following a further re build, it is now called Rowland's Landing).

On another occasion, Sally and Robin witnessed a low flying bomber heading east, skimming the brow of Calamansack hill, Swastikas and Luftwaffe livery plain to see - this time, without discharging bombs!

There are several publications covering Helford in the war, and interested readers are referred to these.

Sources of information.

The core material for this chapter derived from census returns coupled with extracts from the Newspaper archives. The first edition of the book has also provided a substantial framework.
Word of mouth information has provided both new knowledge and corrections. Particular thanks to Sally Thomas, Ronnie Rashleigh, Don Garman, Brian Spargo, and Dee Watt.

Recommended reading: Secret Flotillas: Clandestine sea operations to Brittany, 1940-1944,. (Brooks Richards).

10. Church and Chapel

One of the striking differences between 19th and 21st century Cornwall is the position of religion in mainstream culture. From the 18th century, religion was substantially influenced by John Wesley (1703-1791) , a non conformist theologian and evangelist[1,8]. He was the fifteenth child of a Lincolnshire cleric. Together with his brother Charles, and a fellow preacher George Whitefield, he founded Methodism. He was an ordained clergyman, but aspects of his convictions were outside Church of England creed. His doctrine emphasised the role of religious devotion in daily conduct . He promoted evangelical preaching throughout the country, and encouraged lay preachers to spread the word. John Wesley toured Cornwall in 1745 and visited Falmouth, where he was nearly killed by the mob. But he explained his teachings, and was soon accepted. He revisited the town on four further occasions. A local "society" (regular meeting group) was established, and the seed was sown.

In 1815, a Cornish Methodist lay preacher from Launceston named William O'Bryan began travelling the west country[3]. He was a zealous evangelist spreading the Wesleyan message. He held "Bryanite" meetings in barns, farm kitchens and open fields. and may have been a factor contributing to the fervour with which local communities adopted Methodism into the mainstream. Freedom of religious belief was always permitted by the orthodox church of England, but insisted each county had an Archdeacon who granted and recorded licences for non conformist chapels. Thus the Archdeacon's record provides documented evidence for the development of local Methodism.

"Cove" and Calamansack had been previously served by the Parish Church in Churchtown, Constantine, nearly 3 miles away[4], too far for the less robust walker. Between 1812 and 1821 there was in addition a Methodist meeting house in Constantine. On April 6th 1826, a licence was granted to John Daniel for a new building at Treglidwith to serve as a meeting house. This was the Bryanite chapel at Ponjeravah. It replaced Pascoe's barn of 1824. By 1842[7], Richard Sedwell was granted a licence for a second Bryanite Chapel in a building occupied by Thomas Caddy, farmer of Seworgan in Constantine parish. A year after this licence, a new Methodist chapel was erected in Constantine on a plot owned by Sir Richard Vivyan and leased to the Methodist Society.[5] This is now the Tolmen centre. The Bible Christians united with some other breakaway groups in 1907 to become the united Methodist Church , which by 1929 further combined with the Wesleyan Methodists and Primitive Methodists to become "The Methodist Church". All quite complicated and a little hard to comprehend the politics.

Non Conformists of Port Navas were the majority, and had to attend the Bryanite Chapel at Ponjeravah, over a mile distant, making the village community of this faith somewhat peripheral, and the momentum gathered to have a chapel in the village.

The Mayne family had non conformist leanings, and it seems that William Mayne allowed villagers to use the Seaman's chapel (Mayn Cottage) for Bryanite meetings from early on[3]. In 1868, services were held in the Seaman's chapel at 11.00 a.m. and 5.00 p.m. on Sundays, and at 7.00 p.m. on Wednesdays. The Methodist records show that the number of full members in Cove were :

1851	6 members
1856	11 members
1874	19 members
1906	27 members

In 1878, the Helston circuit report stated: "At Cove, society and congregation have quite outgrown the place" (presumably referring to the Seaman's chapel).

The Bible Christian Magazine of July 1893 reports Cove as follows :
"Cove is a pretty little village in the Parish of Constantine. We have held services in this place for more than forty years, in an inconvenient upper room. There is no other place of worship, church or chapel, nearer than about two miles. There have been various attempts to secure land to build a Chapel, but all attempts have failed until recently. We have now secured a site from Lord Clinton on a 99 year lease. We laid the foundation stones on Friday 2nd June. The stones were laid by Mrs J Harvey of lower town Helston and Mrs S. Tripp of St Keverne. The service in the afternoon was conducted by the Rev. E Rhodes (Wesleyan) and a pastor of the circuit. A goodly number of people from the surrounding neighbourhood were present."

A well attended tea was taken in a nearby tent, and the public meeting was held in the same place. Mr Boaden of Trenarth presided, and addresses were given by Messrs Rhodes, Tripp, Quance and Balkwill.

The chapel was designed to seat ninety people. Many of the other churches showed true interest in the effort, including the Rev James Mayne, a kind hearted clergyman of the neighbourhood. He has given £5.00, and the stones for the building. Thus far we have obtained about £70.00 in cash and reliable promises. The ground rent for the land was to be one shilling per year, payable to Lord Clinton. In 1919, the Trefusis estate sold off their Port Navas interests, and Inow land was bought by Mr William Rowe (son of Mr James Rowe of Mawnan, one of the trustees), to whom the ground rent became payable (recorded in the account ledger for that year. Earlier books are missing).

Building work was mostly undertaken by voluntary labour. In 1894, the Midsummer Quarterly Meeting report announced "The New Chapel at Cove has been opened under encouraging circumstances . The cost of the building including new lamps and labour is about £185, towards which, by collecting books, profit of foundation stone laying and opening services, £131 has been raised." They were lucky that an abandoned building already standing on the ground easily converted into a stable and house for the pony and trap of the visiting minister.

In the previous quarter, the following trustees were appointed for the new Chapel:

William Rashleigh, 74, Famer at Trewince
John Downing, 62, farm labourer at Trenarth Bridge
Steven Bate , 47, Fisherman at Creek Head cottages
Charles Rendle, 34, Oyster dredger, Nancenoy
Joseph Rowe, 51, Farmer from Inow
John Henry Moyle,38, Labourer from Firleigh (Toby Moyle's father).
John Tremayne, 48, Labourer from Inow cottages

The new chapel was opened on Good Friday, March 23rd, 1894. The sermon was delivered by the Rev. J.Stevens, and the new building was packed to capacity. A tent erected in a nearby field accommodated a sit down tea, presided over by Alderman J. Boaden of Mawgan and Trenarth. In the evening, a second service was held, and addressed by the Chairman, Brother Stevens and T. Spillet. The Constantine Wesleyan Choir was in attendance and led the singing. Many could not obtain admission because of the numbers.

The accounts and minutes of the quarterly meetings were retained and make some interesting reading[2]. Expenses on oil, wicks and chimneys for 1894 came to £2 0s 2d. In 1910, 1 cwt coal for heating cost 1s 2d. The annual cleaners wages were £1 13s 4d, and a halter for the pony 6d. There was a plan at one time to demolish the stable, but this was deferred until very recently. Fire cover for 1954 was £1000, and by 1983, £27,000.

On 4th December 1969, a Rhododendron tree was planted to commemorate the 100th birthday of John Stamford Warren, who lived in the cottage opposite. He had helped as a volunteer in the chapel's construction in 1893. In 1992,the chapel purchased the freehold of the site, the money being raised by local subscription. The people of the established church and non conformists in Constantine and Port Navas worked side by side, and without acrimony. The ministers took part in each others services, and the spirit of an Ecumenical community prospered. Improved transport however allowed increasing numbers of the villages worshippers to attend Constantine, and the chapel Congregation began to dwindle. In the 1980's, William Laity, who looked after Inow House garden for Mr Danby, acted as lay preacher. Regular attenders included Mr and Mrs Henry Warren, Mrs Dollar Bruton, Marjorie Tonkin and Arthur Rendle. (Gordon and Marjorie were strictly "Church"). But they all grew older, and eventually were no more. Will Laity moved away. 107 years after its triumphal consecration, neither preacher nor congregation were left. The chapel closed its doors for good in 2011, although Constantine bands "Carolaire" used it in a rainy 2013 With th Reverend Stuart Turner. Gordon Dyer, the last lay preacher, held a Christmas service in the village hall. Like many similar establishments, including the Mayn chapel, it has now been converted into a private house. Progress? As elsewhere, the chapel had sustained human spirits in adverse times, and produced a compassionate and committed community.

69). The New Chapel (top left) about 1924. "Trevean", right, was then the home of Steven and Euphemia Bate, just before Miss Rashleigh bought it.

70). The New Chapel, 1991, with stable on the right.

71). 2015, Stable demolished, the chapel undergoing reincarnation into a very nice private house.

References:

1. John Wesley. His life and work. Lieve
2. Local Chapel Records, loaned by W. Laity esq
3. The People Called Mehodists in Falmouth– Falmouth Central Methodist Church
4. The Bible Christian Jubilee volume 1865
5 History of the parish of Constanine . Henderson 1937
6 Directories in the Cornish Studies Library, Redruth.
7. Tithe map (1842) and Apportionments.CRO
8. The Life of John Wesley.Kenyon

11. Mariners of the busy little port.

Sea going vessels have been used during all stages of the prehistory and medieval past of the Port Navas vicinity (Chapter 3 and Appendix A). Regular trade with European main land had continued since the bronze age, and the role of competent captains was both crucial and highly regarded. Vessels evolved from neolithic wicker and leather construction[1], to bronze age[2] and iron age planked and stitched[3], saxon clench built[4], and similar viking vessels making raids on occasions, medieval cogs[5] and tudor merchants.[6]. Information is readily available , but the emphasis in context with this book is on the 19th and 20th century scene.

 Prior to the transformations in road and rail transport of the19th and 20th century , man used water for the conveyance of all heavy commodities. Small coastal ports, and beaches often with little protection from the weather, were the lifeline for both international and national trade. The sea was a major source of livelihood, and , particularly in the West Country, bred heroic mariners . The sea was always dangerous , claiming many lives and ships. As has been seen, by the mid 19th century, Port Navas became home to a considerable number of master mariners, most of whom had married local girls. From census records there were thirteen resident men holding Masters tickets for either coastal or foreign trade. Included are John and William Rendle, William, Albert and Charles Rendle, William Uden, William Bunt, Stephen and Sydney Bate, Tom Collings, Captains Uden, Thomas, Williams, Box, and Pascoe. Surnames Thomas and Williams suggest Welsh origins, but both were common local names, possibly representing Welsh emigrants associated with coal shipment in the 18th century. In addition to officers and share holders, many other villagers gained a living from sea going vessels. Several of these folk were from Plymouth, engaged in transporting the massive volume of local granite needed for the new naval steam dock. Whether the attraction was the tranquillity of the environment or the girls, is open to speculation! Vessels had to have a significant loading to provide the draft and stability to make a passage, and throughout the commercial period of Port Navas, coal, chalk and limestone were imported, mainly from Newcastle, Wales, and Sussex . Most vessels were returned to their home port for refit between January and March—no worries about rain ruining the varnish. The coating was hot tar!

An exception to the South Devon origins of these seamen were the Bate brothers from Port Isaac, both sons of a mariner, see below). Steven (1855), and Sidney (1857) went to sea together. Sidney was the first to marry. His wife was Jane Kempthorne Bunt, the daughter of Captain William Bunt—himself a managing shareholder in a number of coastal vessels, and resident in the village. Captain Bunt's home was the terrace addition to the Rendle's creek cottage, rented from Ponsaverran. Sidney with his close family connections was part of the Port Navas community, although he later lived in Penryn. Steven Bate married Euphemia Tremayne, daughter of a Port Navas farmer and horse trader, and took over this terraced cottage when Captain Bunt moved away to Mawnan . In 1885, the brothers are reported performing together in a concert held at Ponjeravah school, on the fiddle and accordion. Steven remained in the cottage until he died in 1947 aged 91. The brothers Stephen and Sydney Bate were sons of John Bate (1804), himself a master mariner. The family moved to Padstow and then Rock, from where the boys went to a school at Tredizzic—a two mile walk—and later aged 12 to the Wadebridge Grammar School. During childhood, they saw ship's wrecked on that forbidding coast, but this did not deter the brothers from a life at sea. Age 14, Steven joined his father and older brother Martin aboard the "Pet". Sydney followed later aboard the family schooner "Trebiskin" as cook. Father John Bate was his first skipper, and when he retired, older brother William became master. Sydney worked his way up to AB, and then to master. Eventually he took over command of his father's "Pet ", by now lengthened to 59 tons. He stayed with her for a while, and then joined his brother Steven on "Leurier" (no details of this vessel have been found, and it may be a misspell). Whilst in London, brother Steven fell ill with what was called Rheumatic Fever, and Sydney assumed command for 6 months, until Steven was well enough to return,, Sydney resumed as mate for a few months before he left to get married. H e was offered command of one of Captain Bunt's vessels, "Water Lily". Sidney wrote an account of his seafaring activities, which the Rendle family kept. This monologue of some of his voyages offers wonderful insight into the coastal trading vessels way of life. Herewith an extract from his account, from 1880 to 1881, when he was 23.

"Our next voyage was from Port Navas to Dublin with granite. We made a fast passage, unloaded, took on ballast, and sailed for Garston, where we arrived the following afternoon. Here we loaded coal for Captain Bunt, my father in law, who had a coal business in Port Navas, where we exchanged it for a load of kerb stones for London. Here we took on dog biscuits for Bristol, but were obliged to put in to Padstow on the way, weatherbound. Eventually we got away, and reached Bristol without mishap. From there to Newport, where we loaded coal for Port Navas. We had a rough passage around Land's End, but after taking shelter in Penzance for several days, we reached home safely. It being winter, we stopped running for a couple of months, when we again fitted out and took a cargo of granite coping to Newcastle. We had a record voyage, leaving Port Navas on Thursday, and we were back in three weeks, despite being caught in a gale of wind and having to shelter in Harwich harbour for several days. Going North through Yarmouth Roads, we encountered the impressive sight of four to five hundred sailing ships which had been taking shelter from the storm. We did the whole round trip of 1200 miles, despite our setbacks, including loading and unloading, in exactly three weeks. Having discharged our coal at Port Navas, we took on kerb for London, and from there we loaded cement for Gloucester. I called in home on the way round, and took Janie, my wife, on board for a trip to Gloucester. She greatly enjoyed going up the Gloucester canal. There is a magnificent Cathedral, of which we had a bird's eye view of the outside from the ship. We crossed the Severn to Lydney, Monmouthshire. Here we loaded coal for Port Navas.

72). Could be "Water Lily" aground off Helford point, waiting to discharge coal for Captain Bate's uncle.

Reaching home safely, we discharged some of the coal on Helford beach for my wife's Uncle, Captain T. Bunt, (see photograph) taking the rest home to Port Navas. We next loaded granite for Maryport, and having discharged, loaded pig iron for Pembrey close to Llanelli. We experienced a very heavy gale on our passage to this place, which carried away our main gaff. We fixed the gaff and set a close reefed mainsail, but on running over Llanelly bar, our gaff topsail sheet got fouled in the end of the gaff, so I ran up the rigging, slid out to the peak, halyards, and cleared the sheet. The pilot was at the tiller,. My word! It was a risky bit of work, for had we jibed I would have been flung out to sea. There was a heavy sea running at the time, but sailors do not consider risks when an emergency arises. When we got in, we discharged and reloaded with coal for Messrs Freeman and Sons of Penryn. We had a nice passage home and then loaded granite coping for London. This we discharged at Putney Bridge, but to get there we had to unstep the two masts and lay them on the deck., so we could be towed up under the London Bridges by a small tug.. Afterwards, we were towed to Hay's wharf, where with the aid of a crane, we re-stepped our masts. We towed down to Northfleet near Gravesend, where we took in a cargo of cement, and at the lower reach of Gravesend, we took on 40 tons of powder for Dublin. We had a rather rough voyage there for we were caught in a South Easterly gale in St Georges Channel. We arrived all well, discharged and proceeded to Garston, Liverpool in ballast, where we took on coal for Port Navas I am speaking now of the year 1881, and when we arrived at Garston, we found "Queen of the Chase" with my father in law, Captain William Bunt in command, had just arrived from London with a cargo of ore. We loaded our coal for home, and sailed some days before "Queen of Chase" which was taking on coal for Merthen Hole in the Helford River. We reached home safely. About a fortnight later, I handed over "Water Lily and took over "Queen of the Chase". She was built in Falmouth by James

Mayn for Pope and Co, and lengthened in 1862 to 98.02 tons. The Popes ran fast fruit ships as well as other cargoes and she had been in both the Mediterranean and also the Newfoundland trades. Edwin Pope tried to sell her in 1880, but she failed to make a reserve price. Captain Bunt of Port Navas owned her between 1886 and We loaded kerbing at the lower quay, Port Navas, for Dover. The wind was blowing hard from the East, and so we waited a few days till it changed to South West and I made up my mind to sail. It was in the afternoon, and my wife had read in the newspaper that a gale from America , was predicted to sweep across the Atlantic, so she did not want me to set off. I had made up my mind to do so, and we left Helford on the Thursday afternoon in the latter part of September. The next day about 5 p.m. we were caught in the predicted gale off St Catherine's Point, Isle of Wight.

The gale struck us all of a sudden. We were running with single reefed sails, when without any warning the wind veered North and struck the ship with great force carrying away the jib boom, boom, jip and all the gear attached, which fell into the ea. The main sheet carried away and the main boom swung out and hit the after shroud of the main rigging. I immediately put her head up to wind, and urged the crew to cut the wreckage adrift before the jib boom could knock a hole in our bow. Whilst we were in this predicament, a large steamer proceeding down channel, al- tered course and came close to us. The Captain through a megaphone, asked if we required any help. I replied that so far we were in no danger as our vessel was not making any water. I thanked him for approaching so closely to find out if we needed assistance.

After a couple of hours, we got the wreckage free, and keeping the "Queen of the Chase" hove to, we had our tea, which included a blackberry pie, which my wife had made for us to take to sea.

We remained hove to till midnight, when the gale moderated somewhat. I then sailed her under close reefed canvas to Dover, which we reached on Sunday without further trouble..

At Dover we loaded cement for somewhere on the Medway and then sailed for Liver- pool again with a further cargo of cement. When we were off Newhaven the ship was caught in another very heavy Nor'westerly gale and we had to run to Dungeness Roads for shelter. At midnight the wind backed and blew hurricane force from W.S.W.

Both cables were out to their full extent and we had them shackled to the mast. A Dutch pilot boat was blown clean out of the roads. The next morning I beheld a ves- sel completely disabled, sails blown away being driven helplessly before the gale.

After a couple of days, the wind subsided enough for us to resume our passage west- ward. We put in to Portland for the night.

We left the next day, but after a few hours the wind blew very hard from the East and as she was making water, we decided to put in to Falmouth for repairs. She was beached at Boyer's Cellars and the Shipwrights found that she needed some caulk- ing. We left the next day and reached Land's End . Thirty six hours later we reached Liverpool and discharged the cement."

Describing another occasion when he had to deal with mountainous seas and a shifting cargo, he tells how they managed at last to reach the entrance to Port Navas creek where his father in law was just hauling his nets with a load of herring. Capt. Bunt said he was most surprised to see them as he had given them up for lost. "Queen of the Chase" was the only vessel out of nearly three hundred which had reached her destination. All the rest had either taken shelter, put in for repairs, or were lost. "My wife was agreeably surprised to see me" he said. "She had been asking her father where he thought they had gone. Other anecdotes include a close encounter with a barque bearing down on them. "**Queen of the Chase"** was on passage to Queenstown when the other vessel was seen to be on a collision course. Captain Bates took avoiding action, but the ship followed him, so he fired a gun. The officers came on deck and relieved the apprentice at the helm, and tragedy was avoided. His wife and 6 week old son were on board, and they became seasick following the incident. On another occasion, "Queen of the Chase" and "Howard" (Capt William Rendle) loaded salt together in Penryn for Newlyn. They unloaded there together, and both took on broken stone for Cardiff, sailing in company. The "Queen" arrived in the morning, and the "Howard" in the evening. They docked in the West Dock together, unloaded and both took on coal for Helford. "The Queen " was loaded and departed two days earlier than "Howard", and was home for Christmas. Bad weather prevented "Howard" from making port before the end of the first week of January 1880.

The above account gives insight into the speed at which new freights were commissioned— shipping agents had needed a substantial network of traders, and the Master had to handle all necessary paper work and accounts. During this period, "Queen of the Chase" was still owned by Edwin Pope, having failed to meet her reserve at auction in 1880. After Sydney Bate relinquished command in 1881, she was skippered by Captain Webster. In 1886 she sat on her anchor off Greenbank in Falmouth and flooded. In 1887 Captain Webster broke his leg when the ship's tow hawser snapped. Sydney Bates eventually bought her, and became owner skipper. In April 1905 she was sheltering off Cardiff. Two of his sons were with him. She capsized on Cardiff Sands and became a constructive total loss. The figurehead was recovered, and was sold in 2012 at a London auction (see appendix 1).

Captain Tom Collings (1866-1947), from Bude, married Elizabeth Jane Exelby (of Pennance) and lived in Mayne Cottage from 1911. He owned shares in ships, and also imported coal. He skippered the schooner "Guiding Star" (1871, 107 tons) through the First World War. She was lightly armed, and carried gun crews. In Winter she used to lay up, stern to, under the Lime Kiln. He retired from the sea after the war, and his ship was taken over by Captain Keats of Port Isaac, but continued to winter in her old berth in the creek, where her former master could keep an eye from Mayn Cottage. (There must be a photograph in someone's attic!) In the early 1920's he took over the running of the shop from Steven Bate. "Guiding Star" foundered off Ballycotton in April 1928 after a heavy sea damaged her bulwarks and hatches in an Easterly Gale. The story is told in the Western Morning News of April 19th that year.

94

It is salutary to reflect on the super human effort required to work these vessels. Crews were minimal. Danger was a constant companion at sea, costing the lives of many men. Most ships were eventually lost. Officers and ordinary seamen had to share the work —watch keeping, sail changing, helming and maintenance. In port stevedores were not always available, and in any case, speed of turnaround, meant they had to engage in cargo changing . These were the days before Telephone, Radio or useable Forecasts. Instinct and the barometer had to serve. Few Captains owned their own homes ashore, and life for the family was unthinkably tough by modern values. All in a day's work. As in chapter 12, religious conviction was at the heart of the community lifestyle, and a crucial driver. They were mostly Wesleyans, which is reflected in the name they gave to the basin at the creek entrance— Abraham's Bosom. Some married local girls, others retired to Port Navas. In those days, the village was strongly represented by mariners, with the wisdom associated with first hand experience of the sea in all its moods. Few could afford to buy their own house, and pensions hadn't been invented.

Over 100 years, it is likely 2000 trading vessels discharged or took on cargo in Port Navas. A comprehensive list is impossible because no port records survive, but many names can be gathered from Shipping News reports in the 19th and 20th centuries. Based in Port Navas include:
"Howard", "Water Lily", "Queen of the Chase", "Millie", "Rob Roy", "Sunbeam", "Guiding Star" and **"VB Lamb".**
Known visitors and some cargos include:**"Pet",**1871, **"Trebiskin"**, granite 1873, **"Leurier"** granite, 1874, **"Iris"** *1875"*, "**Lady of Avenel,** granite , 1876, *"***Swallow",** *s*tone, *1878,* **"Ethel Jane",** 1880, **"RGD"** coal, Nov 1895, . **"Siren"** coal, 1896, . **"Sir Francis Drake",** Bideford, coal, (After discharging coal at Port Navis, driven ashore Gedges May 1898. She was refloated, and continued in trade.). *"***Duchess"** Coal, *1929,* **"Fanny Crossfield"** coal 1936, **"Result"** , coal. For more see Appendix A

73). *Grave of John Doyle from Carlow, drowned with four others when the previous ketch "Trebiskin" was wrecked off Worm's Head, April 1918*

References:
1. Britain Begins, Barry Cunliffe, 2014
2. The Ships of Sea People part 2. J. Thomas
3. The Atlantic Iron Age. Jon Henderson, 2007
4. Guernsey Museum Rports.
5. Mariners, Merchants and the Military too. Philip Jones
6. Medieval Ship Types. Alsford 2006
7.Elizabethan merchant Ships and Shipbuilding. Ian Friel, 2009

12. Post World War Two to 20 15

Following the hostilities, Port Navas gradually returned to normal. The principal employment remained agriculture, with a few members of the village working in Falmouth docks. A range of trades flourished along the quay road. Toby Moyle ran his carpentry business from the workshop under his house, Skip Thomas built an excellent reputation as a motor and marine engineer, and Graham Rogers had his boat repair yard on the upper quay. The Duchy oyster farm continued to thrive, owned by Unilever, and under the management of Sid Hodges junior. But no more cargo vessels called. Occasional stone barges were brought to the lower quay, and may account for the two blocks which went from there after 1930 (page 71). Howard Rendle had taken over as River Pilot from his father Albert, but his services were only required for occasional coal and grain cargo vessels to Richard's wharf at Gweek, apart from the Royal visit in 1968. One vessel to visit was "Result", a steel three masted schooner, now preserved at the Ulster Folk and Transport Museum.

Ronnie Rashleigh worked with Graham Rogers for six years between 1944 and 1952, having previously learned his trade as a shipwright and carpenter with Falmouth Boat Construction during the war. He then lived in a converted gypsy caravan on the upper quay. Sally Thomas trained as a nurse, and worked as Orthopaedic Theatre sister , and in the Resuscitation Unit for A&E at the Royal Cornwall Infirmary, Truro ("the City"). Her brother Robin became a textile designer and teacher at Bristol University. He also worked in costume departments of stage and TV. He eventually took Holy Orders and had the living at Tintagel. Betty and Michael Danby grew up at Inow House, Dee Watt at Rose Hill Cottage, and Phillip Webber at Ponsaverran. They have the best first hand knowledge of the village in the 1950's, and all have generously contributed to this account.

Graham Rogers sold the quay to partners Eric Bannister and Harold Penrose in 1941, but continued to run the business until 1951. Mr Penrose, became head of Westland helicopters. Ronnie Rashleigh left in 1952, to work in the docks. Eric Bannister was the active partner on the quay, and continued to run a "yacht" yard, although this was an excessive description of what, by then, were mainly boats. On the quay he built a house over a workshop in 1950 , now converted to two holiday flats.

Nearly every household had a local wage earner. Before the war, the Hodges had moved into the old pub, re christened "Chestnut Cottage". There were father and son, both called Sidney. The family remained in occupation for nearly 40 years. Sidney Hodges the younger was head of the household in 1950, and Len succeeded his father as manager of the oyster farm in 1953—the third generation of the family to manage the business. Len and Erica with their two children Lindsey and Brenda occupied the new extension, and Len's sister and parents were in the original pub. Macfisheries put major investment into the Oyster farm, which underwent a rebuild (see picture). It attracted a succession of distinguished visitors, including Prince Charles, as well as an annual visit by the directors of Unilever.

74). Spring c. 1950. Graham Rogers had been busy building sheds. The structure to the left of the quay, on the site of the former granite gantry is an adapted gypsy caravan, subsequently the site of the first asbestos club house. It was home to Ronnie Rashleigh , and later Norman Mummery. Behind this is another shed, where previously a scrap bus had served as Graham's office. Yet another new shed (to the right of the caravan) survives today, and was used as a workshop by Tim Rendle. The smithy shop has been extended, and a further shed has appeared abutting the back wall of the yard (still there). Site of Eric Bannister's new house out of view, but not yet built.

Both Captains Steven Bates and Tom Collings died in 1947, followed by Mrs "Zoe" Collings in 1952. Oliver Thomas, Fred's brother, then moved down from Kent into Mayne Cottage. He died in 1958, and had expressed a wish to be interred in his native county. Toby Moyle was engaged to make the coffin and do the necessary. He took the coffin to Truro Station in Fred's truck, and assisted putting it on the train. "Mind," he said, "he'll have to change at Paddington".

Farmer White, running Ponsaverran Farm, lived in Ponsaverran Farmhouse (now called ChyanDowr). He retired in 1954 when the tenancy was taken over by Joselyn Ratcliffe of Argal, a solicitor and land owner. Harold Rickard was engaged as manager, and later became independent tenant. His herd of milking Guernseys sometimes grazed on the fore field above the lower quay – a wonderful sight.

Living in "Croft Cottage" was widowed Mrs Tremayne with her daughter, and her niece Millie next door in "Rose cottage". The Rendles at "the Cottage" comprised Eva Jane, widow, of Albert (1869-1936), Gordon (a purser on P&O passenger liners), and twins Arthur and Marjorie. Gordon's fishing boat was called **"Eva Jane"**. Arthur worked for Skip Thomas (see chapter 9), and Marjorie became a trained nurse and ran the casualty department in Truro Hospital. Oldest son and war hero Howard had married Dot, and built "Up Along", above Millie Tremayne.

Miss Bessie Isaac lived in the end cottage. Henry Warren and his wife moved into the second terraced cottage at the creek head. He worked for the oyster farm, as did his brother Tiny, and Stan Williams from the cottages up the hill.

Eric Bannister and a group of business friends, including John Harris, Mike Wilkins, and a Mr Ohlenslagger (who was subsequently killed in the Angel, Helston) erected a temporary asbestos hut on the site of the present club (see photograph). Norman Mummery was the first "host" and club manager, occupying the gypsy caravan (above). He was a charming bachelor, and a serious alcoholic, which later became his undoing. A dispute arose with the authorities when the group were believed to have omitted planning, including erecting the hut. The ground floor of the new house was then deployed, and titled "Yacht Yard Club for members only". In 1966 Tim Rendle, Howard's son, opened a workshop in the quayside shed which Graham Roger's had built. He had trained as a shipwright in Plymouth. (The shed is still there , Tim not).

Meanwhile conflict erupted between village residents and commerce. In 1955, three Vinnicombe brothers required a base for their marine salvage operation, and took a lease on the lower quay from the Reverend Webber, then owner of Ponsaverran. A number of wreck sites litter Falmouth Bay, but the particular interest was **"SS Volnay"** off Porthallow. She was a 4,610grt, 285ft long defensively-armed British Merchant Ship. On the 14th December 1917 inbound from Montreal for Plymouth she hit a mine 2 miles E by S of the Manacles. (German mines were a recognised hazard off the Lizard). While attempting to beach her at Porthallow, she foundered in 70 ft, a mile from the shore. She had anti personnel shells in the hold, whose brass cases and shot are still found at the site today. The Vinnicombes used a deep draft retired Lowestoft steam drifter as salvage vessel. They later acquired the shallow draft **"VB Lamb"** (see appendix) , They also ran as support vessel a fine teak built 35 ft ex tripper launch, **"Freelance"** There was a wonderful time when children could pick up buckets of cordite from mountains left exposed on the quay -great for making rockets out of bicycle pumps. Health and Safety would have had a fit! Then the **"VB Lamb"** sprang a leak in her plating, and settled alongside the quay, where she was scrapped. Marine salvage and the scrap industry were never tidy, and the gentle folk of the village started a campaign to remove the entire enterprise. The Vinnicombes proposed opening a café instead, but were deemed to have insufficient experience to make this an asset. The hearing reached national press coverage. For want of a better word, the Nimby's won. The Vinnicombes received £15,000 compensation, and a discontinuance order for commercial use was imposed. On a personally felt note, the three brothers made off with a third Pennance painted lady. She had formally graced the tea gardens, and had been donated to the club, intended to greet visitors on the quay. She took an undignified and exhausting wheel barrow journey from Pennance to the club, where her first stop was a pint at the bar, where she passed virtually unnoticed—a tribute to the quality of the beverage available. She was last seen for sale in Vinnicombe's recycling yard in Penryn. Shame!

Brian Spargo is a modest hero of the village where he has lived all his life. A true Cornishman, in his working life he served time with Skip Thomas at the garage, worked with the Vinnicombes in marine salvage , and latterly worked at Wheal Jane, and then South Crofty tin mines before they were finally closed. The latter 400

75). Mayn cottage 1951. The widowed Mrs Elizabeth Collings (nee Exelby) with cat. The doorway on the left was an entrance to Freeman's office.

76). Skip Thomas's garage, Summer 1960s. Note petrol Pumps, Skip's Rover 60, Firleigh and Shearwater (centre).

77). Brian Spargo, the last resident tin miner in the village. His family have probably been involved in stone masonry, granite quarrying and mining for at least 200 years.

78).Walter Warren outside his general store, 1960s. The freezer was always stocked with fish he had caught off the Manacles.

Sadly, competition from the super markets undermined local custom, and they had to close. Another example of "Use it or lose it".

79). Creek head about 1961. Sally Thomas's dinghy moored in background under Firleigh. White motor boat is Walter Warrens, (his brothers Henry and Tiny also had identical boats, one of which is lent to port built by Willie Johns. Toby Moyle's grandson sitting on red pram in foreground. This originally belonged to the oyster farm.

80). Creek head late 1960s. Blue motor boat is "Seaman", built by Dick Winfrey. On the right is "Tern", built by Willie Johns of Flushing, 1934. He also built many local motor boats ,3 owned by the Warrens. Mike Wilkinson's ASR launch alongside the quay.

81). Constantine band rehearsing "Carolaire". 1980s

year old mine pursued lodes of tin extending 2 1/2 miles, and descended to 3,000 ft. Brian is thus, uncontested, the last tin miner to live in the village. He has taken a great interest in local history, and owns a fine collection of photographs several of which are reproduced here. He was born (as were his mother Mildred and her twin sister Doris) in his grandfather Rowling's cottage at Lower Goongillings- the old blow house for Wheal Caroline tin mine. He lives in a house three doors from that in which he grew up, at Inow Terrace. Sadly his wife Sally recently passed away. Brian's father, Hugh, worked in Bosahan quarry, and later for the council on the highways. James Spargo, a stone mason, lived at Lower Calamansack in 1841 and 1851. He appears to be related, his father being Brian's three times great grandfather. So the family name persists locally since that time.

Herbert Warington Smyth's widow Amabel continued to live in Calamansack after her husband died in 1941. Their oldest son Bevil married a Californian girl, Barbara (Bobby) Menzies, in 1938. They had two daughters, Pin and Dee. Sadly Bevil died in 1951, and Bobby, Pin and Dee lived in Rose Hill Cottage, next door to Grandma Amabel, The cottage was owned by the Duchy. When Grandma died in 1968, they moved up to Calamansack, and Len and Erica Hodges took the lease at Rose Hill, and moved in. It is now the home of Rear Admiral Sir Robert Woodard, previously master of the Royal Yacht Britannia, who has kindly written a forward to this book. Dee married John Watt, and ran a smallholding in Coombe for some years. They recently moved back to Port Navas, much to local delight. Apart from the pleasure of seeing locals back in the community, the Warington Smyth connection is a reminder of the strong mining and geological associations. In addition to Herbert Warington Smyth, Port Navas has two other distinguished geologists connected with the village. David Bruton, was until recently, Professor at the Museum of Natural History in Oslo, Norway, and is best known for his work on the Burgess Shale fossils. He grew up in Shearwater with his mother Dollar and brother Michael. His son still has land up Trewince Lane, and Michael now owns Shearwater. Both brothers return most years. Professor Peter Scott is the third distinguished geologist, and lives in the village currently. He was previously Head of Geology at Camborne School of Mines (chapter 7). Nobody is better informed over local geology, and I am very grateful for his contribution to this book.

John and Dee Watt still own the Warington Smyth family boat "Campion", a handsome 18ft clinker built vessel built by the "Falmouth Boat Construction" in 1948, and designed by Dee's father Bevil. David Handley of Lower Calamansack owns the sister ship "Mary Jane", as well as the gaff cutter "Otter", which is undergoing restoration. This lovely 35ft 1915 Fowey built vessel was bought by the Myers family in 1954 for £200, and has been a feature of the river ever since. Tony and Sue Myers bought Trewince Country House in 1945 from Mr and Mrs Gealer (chapter 9). They ran it as a popular and highly successful hotel and restaurant for the next 30 years. Their children Jane, and Rodney usually attend the Port Navas regatta. Sally Ann now, lives in New Zealand.

102

Leonard Knibb, an engineer from London, bought the derelict Penpoll Mill in 1951, and started the present works. The watermill had been inactive after World War One. In 1958, Len married Irene Kerslake (nee Thomas), a vicar's widow who was then running Rose Cottage tea garden in Helford, with her teenage son David. When Len died in 1985, Irene and David, then a merchant seaman, decided to continue the business, which became "I. Knibb and Son" - a courageous step. It is the biggest business in Port Navas by a considerable margin , with a workforce of 15. Currently the firm mainly undertake work for Exsel Pumps of Southampton.

The next occupants of Calamansack have also had a major impact. John Green grew up in Norfolk in a family of architects. With his brother, he founded a very successful agricultural business in Ely. "Green's of Soham" continues to thrive. He married Margaret Dixon in 1964, and they adopted the Helford River as a holiday destination, and rented part of Calamansack House. They bought Calamansack in 1979, and moved down permanently in 1995. John founded the Helford River Children's Sailing Trust, based on the banks of Abraham's Bosom below the ancient oak woods of Calamansack . The Trust is a blend of Arthur Ransomesque boating, with a flavour of Breton Ecole de Voile, and very successful. John was awarded an MBE for his contribution. Sadly he died in 2014, but Margaret remains at Calamansack.

 Henry Warren left the oyster farm, and moved up to Inow Terrace, tending the garden for the Mangeons at Treetops. The middle terrace cottage at the creek head became available. It was taken over by Stan Williams who worked at the oyster farm, and was then re developed when Miss Isaac left the end terrace. The two terraced cottages as one home are now billet for ex naval officer James Lucas and his wife Annabelle. Over two decades, they became central figures "down town". Annabelle spent her early years at Drift with her grandmother. James is now in a nursing home, but Annabelle remains involved with many local activities.

Another well known name of the 1950s is Diana Wynyard, who lived in Oyster House. Originally built by Mr and Mrs Parker in the 1930s it has a fabulous view of the creek. She was a film and stage star, whose career stretched from 1932 to 1964, the year she died. She starred with John Gielgud, Michael Redgrave and Maggie Smith. It After Miss Winyard, the house was bought by Commander George Heppel. It is now the home of Tim Taylor who created the BBC's "Time Team" programme.

Inow House (see Mortimer, chapter 8) was bought in 1939 by Jack Silley, the owner of Falmouth Repair Docks as well as Repair docks on the Thames. He had pioneered mass production of ship building in World War one. He died at Inow in 1943, but his son and family remained during the war years, and his grand children grew up with Sally and Robin Thomas. In 1945 the house was on the market, and bought, together with the terrace of cottages on the road, by Edward Danby, a retired farmer from India. He moved in with his wife and two children, Michael and Betty, and remained there until he died in 1980, aged 100 . His father was a Yorkshire cleric who had married into the Baddeley family. They were the owners of 2 Indian Indigo farms, a popular and successful enterprise for colonials in the 19th century. Edward Danby had gone out to the colonies as farm manager in 1897. The Danby family also owned Penare House near Porthallow, where they were all staying when war was declared. Edward returned to India, but his wife and two small children stayed behind in

82). Creek head 1956. "Birowlie", our family motor boat, with Stuart Turner engine. Bought from Edward Danby, and named after one of their Indian Indigo Farms. The Rendle flatty dinghy in the foreground, and transom of Harold Rickard's motor boat on the right. Obscured is Henry Warren's boat.

83). Port Navas creek 1960s.. "Otter" in the foreground, Vinnicombe brothers "Freelance" off the quay.

84).Good and great of the village, 2010

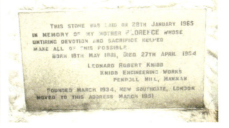

Trenarth Bridge, Knibbs Engineering. Clockwise from top left:
85). Penpoll Mill, originally one of four grist mills in Bosaneth stream, which was culverted alongside the road to drive the mill wheel. There are also "Penpoll Mills" in Feock and Bodmin.
86.) The old mill house gable is part of the present factory. Bought by Len Knibb and his mother Florence in 1951, he transferred his engineering business here from New Southgate, Barnet.
87.) This memorial stone to Len Knibb's mother Florence is on the wall of the same wall . Len Knibb married widowed Iris Kerslake in 1956. When he died, she and her son David took on the business.
88.) I.Knibb & Sons engineering is , and has been for 65 years, the biggest employer in the village, with With an impressive number of sophisticated, machine tools, and a workforce of 15, output fills a lorry weekly. In a competitive world, it has been an enduring success, and is an outstanding achievement.

England, until the farms were sold in 1943, and he returned. He joined Kerrier Council, which he chaired during the 1950's. Betty went to Oxford in 1949, , somewhat to her father's chagrin. There she encountered a young Cornish born Naval officer, John Edwards. He had been invalided out of the service with a lung ailment. They married in Falmouth in 1950, and returned to Port Navas. John formed a partnership with William Gunton, and they established a much respected estate agents. They took a lease on the old shop and post office which had stood unused for some time. Gunton and Edwards Office was a prominent feature of the village centre in the 1950s and 60s. The Edwards were great sailors. When John retired, the office, (originally Steven Bate's post office), became the "Save the Children" charity shop, much to the delight of the young and not so young, who loved delving through the range of treasures on sale. It was run by a retired colonial nurse, Mary Hawkins, who was awarded an MBE for her services. John Edwards died in 1998, and Betty re married to Nick Williams a widower, who was the retired head of Burma Oil. Sadly Nick has also now died, but Betty continues to live in Constantine. Recently Nick William's son Giles acquired the quay and Lime Kiln. We are all delighted, and wish him well. The importance to the community of retaining the club cannot be overstated. It has been a centre piece of the village for over 60 years, sometimes against the odds. Currently it is possibly serving the best food ever. It enjoys a wonderful aesthetic position, at the heart of our industrial past. It has had a succession of hosts, notably Patrick and Liz Scribbens, and more recently Peter and Margaret Goad. It is a wonderful asset for keeping the community together. Like so many villages in a changing culture, we no longer have a chapel, and the club needs the full support of the community.

Widow Tremayne of the horse trading family died in Croft Cottage in 1953. Croft cottage was sold, and finally was bought in 1956 by Robert and Gwen Gardiner. They had a clothing businesses in Barnet and Eastbourne , which they handed over to their sons Stuart and Michael. The family name has remained at Croft ever since. Dilys came to Port Navas in 1973, when she married Stuart. As newly weds, they lived in Stuart's wooden bungalow Dinyan, built by Frank Honey in the 1930s (see chapter 9). It had always been intended to build a new house on the same site, but in 1979, events intervened. Whilst the council pest controllers were attempting to evacuate a swarm of bees, the place was destroyed by a fire. Stuart and Dilys moved back to "Croft Cottage" which had been unused after Stuart's parents had died, and Dilys has been there ever since, now with Geoff Bird. She is a bedrock of most happenings in the village. Because of her many interests, she always knows what is going on, even if she is away on safari! Few days pass without seeing Roger Macdonald or his father Bruce heading down to or returning from the creek, always offering a helping hand. Roger trained as a helicopter pilot in the Navy, and remained at Culdrose as a flying instructor after leaving the service. Both father and son are avid sailors, and particularly involved in supporting young people on the water

The community is very active, because key people make it so. Many names deserve mentioning, but a few inclusions are essential. In particular, acquisition of the former wash house and reading room, built originally for the village by Ambrose Mayne in 1904. Led by the late Tom Cross, this involved a major fund raising effort, which began in 2001. It was purchased from Philip Webber in 2002, and given charitable status, with trustees Tom Cross, Mike Ford, Fiona Beale, Margaret Scott, Dilys Gardiner, Sally Thomas, Brian Roper and Chris Ohly. A Lottery grant enabled refurbishment to proceed, and the formal opening was undertaken by the High Sheriff of Cornwall, Christopher Perkins in March 2003 . The committee has been chaired by Caroline McDonald, Jim Boote and Margaret Scott. The village hall is a great bonus, run by a band of gallant volunteers. There is an excellent programme of evening meetings through the winter, art exhibitions, coffee mornings, courses on a range of topics, and private functions. Particular credit goes to David Burke, Sally Thomas, Jeff and Tiff Meadows , Roger and Bernice Wickens and Margaret Scott for this continuing success.

One of the major events of the annual calendar is Regatta day. The first official regatta was held in 1914, although previous water celebrations had occurred. Suspended during the first world war, and re introduced in 1922, it happened in most of the between war years. It was re instated again in 1962, around the lower quay and Fore field, through Philip Webber's generosity.

It is a sizeable event, involving enormous effort from the organising committee, which is currently chaired by Richard Tiptaft, a retired urologist from the London Hospital, who lives at Point Cottage. Sally Thomas and Dilys Gardiner are permanent members of the committee.

Art has been a lifelong personal interest, and the area abounds with talent, of which some is included in this book. We are very proud of Tom Cross (see above). A highly regarded professional painter, he was head of the Falmouth Art School. He and his wife Pat moved into Dinyan after its rather protracted rebuild to a new architect design, where the former "Tire me Out" became his studio. As well as driving the village hall project, he was a key contributing stimulus to the regular art exhibitions held in the hall and the local art group with weekly meetings.

Our busy little port of the 19th century has lost most of its commercial side, although thriving businesses remain, with Henry Collins farming, Ben Wright with Oysters, and David Kerslake of I. Knibb and Son .

Tourism never really took off. Tripper boats no longer visit the lower quay, and if they were to do so, would be chased off by Messrs Wright who are running a commercial operation. Anyway nobody is currently likely to serve them tea. Perhaps Port Navas mud has a limited appeal for tourists, but Port Navas wouldn't be the same without it. Silting is a phenomenon in most rivers and creeks. The valleys of Port Navas and the main river were originally created by erosion from wind, ice and storm water rush, but when sea levels are stable as at present, beach platforms form offshore, with sand bars below the surface. This slows currents, and increases precipitation. Many activities have been blamed for our mud, including mining detritus, and increased disturbance with powered agriculture. But mud sedimentation is an inevitable consequence of natural erosion. With sufficient storm water and tidal scour, nature finds a balance. Hand digging of mud from the edge of the upper quay is said to explain the bank of mud between the quay and Dinyan. The problem does not really seem much worse now than in the 1875 photograph of "Lady of Avenel" (page 46). The club pontoon moorings possibly baffle the natural scour, and could accelerate local silting. Maybe if neglected, ultimately it could leave the little fleet of pleasure craft marooned on alluvium. Some ecologists hold very strong views on dredging or water blasting, and this makes it difficult to gain approval for active interventions. However, the increased rainfall predicted with global warming and El Nino events should sort it out. Mind you, the climate pundits say sea levels are on the rise again. Is this the moment to approach the council about sea defences? Anyway, we haven't run out of Port Navas mud just yet.

Once seemingly permanent fixtures of the community, such as the Warrens, Rendles, Westlakes, Dollar Bruton, Millie Tremayne, Sue and Tony Myers, Fiona Beale , Stan Williams, the Tonkins, Ogdens, and Shaws, are no longer with us. Some members of their families return on visits. The two Miss Harrisons have also now passed on. Daughters of a jeweller and pawnbroker from Middlesex, they moved to Devon before the war, and stayed as paying guests with the Trerice's at Trenarth. Hilda lived to 98, and Dorothy became the third centenarian in the village (commonplace it seems—must be something in the water!).

Infill building and development have transformed the village I remember when I first knew it in the 1930s over 80 years ago. The place existing now is the result of the hard graft of people then. Most homes were rented. The charm of the area has stimulated a lot of new building , sometimes in an austere environment, and more in affluent times. New developments never please every taste, and are usually controversial, but there is no doubt that it has insidiously altered the character of the original attraction. I would be upset if change comes via a distant speculator focusing on computerised business charts, with little regard for local life. But we have to accept change. I suppose, so called "progress" now is really no different from the impact of the Mayns in the 19th century, or even more so, arrival of man in the neighbourhood 10,000 years ago.

Crucially thus far, Port Navas has mainly avoided becoming a ghost town, owned by wealthy absentees, who see the properties like pieces on a monopoly board, ignoring the community. But that fate has ruined many Cornish picture villages, and the risk is ever present here. Port Navas has become a popular retirement area, but recently younger people with children are appearing as year round residents— four babies born in the last five years! Very good news, and long may it continue.

Stories and fact from the past are always of interest when they relate to a place which is imbedded in one's soul, but few can claim iron age settlements on their doorstep. The place has attracted achieving people, past and present which make up this story are truly extraordinary. big medieval estates were mostly owned and administered by absentee gentry, which clouds our understanding of their communities, but the Mayne family bucked that trend. Genuine locals for centuries, 200 years ago they transformed the neighbourhood and created a beautiful village. The wharves have shipped iconic granite components of our nations heritage. Port Navas can boast many great lives, in a wide variety of fields. Industrial leaders seem almost two a penny, and include oil, pharmaceuticals, aviation, ship building and retail. The village has made significant contributions to both 20th century war efforts. Past and present, we have associations with four world renowned geologists, and two admirals, and two knights of the realm. Even heirs to the throne have shown more than a passing interest.

Outstanding local businesses include Knibb's engineering, Oyster farming, the winner on points of the best pub in the country at Trengilly, and, I suppose, an unusually high score in residents who become centenarians!

Port Navas is exceptional not just for its accumulation of human achievements. In this beautiful setting, it is also a haven for nature. Ospreys are breeding, there are kingfisher partners in the creek, grey mullet forage on the food tide, heron, seagulls and waders grace mud flats.at low water, and the circadian rhythm of the tide provides an ever changing vista. Although tidal bores are reported, the Lizard acts as guardian from excesses of weather and tsunami.

Who could ask for anything more? We have little, if anything to complain about, and are incredibly lucky to live here! When the first edition was published in 1994, many of the events in chapter 12 had yet to happen! I wonder what would be added in another two decades or so.

Port Navas and its community will continue to flourish for as long as the folk who live here contribute, and take a pride in its guardianship.

Chapter 12. Sources and References.

The Book of Constantine (Trethowan and Moore, 2000) is a treasure trove of anecdote and information, and has provided much material . Newspaper archives and Registries of Births, Marriages and Deaths have also been incorporated where appropriate.

As in Chapter 9, heavy reliance has been placed upon first hand knowledge, and personal communication. Advices and corrections from the extensive list on page 4 have been the linchpin, without which the book would not have reached fruition.

Appendix A: Ships based in or associated with the Port.

Humans and their predecessor hominids have used boats in one form or another for at least 100,000 years. By the iron age, sewn plank hulls had replaced dugout log boats, or Neolithic hide covered vessels. Falmouth Maritime Museum has examples.

Prehistoric trading vessels likely to have visited Helford

89). Competing in Port Navas regatta 3,500 B.C. (courtesy of Ron Prior)
Sea going hide and wicker curragh like vessels plied regular trade across the channel. Continental trade included shipping livestock. (Cunliffe). Vessels up to 45 ft long were built inverted, using long hazel poles bent into a series of arches as frames, bound together with vines, with split hazel, wicker woven between. The frame was covered with animal hides. Light, strong, and efficient! Local artifacts suggest such seamen visited our area.

90).Bronze age (3000-1150 B.C.), Regular cross channel trade was prevalent in late Bronze age. The model left is based on a wreck site at Ulubrum,urkey. It measured 50ft L.O.A., with a 20 ton capacity, carvel planked. Equivalent vessels were employed in the cross channel trade.

91). Romano Gallic merchant vessel, 55—400 A.D. (courtesy Fran Stuart, and based on the Guernsey wreck, which was about 66ft LOA and 20ft beam) It is certain such vessels came to Helford..They often went via Scilly, where 300+ broach offerings were left on Nornour.

92). Visiting Saxon and Norse/ Viking clenched built vessels (500—1000 A.D). This is an armed vessel, although the Cornish were normally in cahoots with Vikings. Trading vessels were known as Knaars. Up to 70ft, 17 ft beam and capable of carrying 20tons + across the Atlantic.

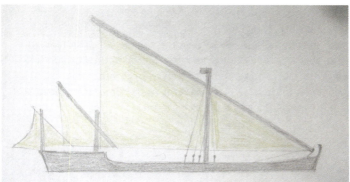

93). 14th century lateen rigged merchant. Such vessels plied trade the length of the channel (Courtesy Shirley Knowles

94). Tudor Merchant Vessel. Up to 90 ft LOA. Such craft would certainly have called here in their day. LOA 60ft. The 16th century river would have matched the present, and been easily recognised.

111

19th Century. Port Navas wharves are likely to have averaged a minimum of 50 vessels berthing per year for 90+ years, totalling about 5,000 arrivals and departures. Sadly, no Port registry survives, and the best sources of information are from newspaper archives, and other ad hoc reports. Here are notes on 20 vessels known to have used Port Navas.

"Lady of Avenel", 163 tons, Length 99.2, beam 23ft. Brigantine rigged.

Builder HS Trethowan, Falmouth 1874, for the Granite trade. She also served in the Newfoundland trade.
She is the most widely known of vessels which used Port Navas.
Rescued by Captain Wilfred Dowman after WW 1, she served as a training ship and was based in both Falmouth and Bridlington, from where she made a voyage to Spitzbergen. He sold her when he bought Cutty Sark in 1922. She then became support vessel for the British Arctic expedition 1925, and reached 89 degrees North. She later attended King George 6th Coronation review in 1938. Finally laid up in Poole before the war, she was vandalised and sank in the mud. Her figurehead survives, in Germany, and the binnacle is in Poole museum. She inspired a brigantine rigged steel training ship of the same name, which remains in commission.
A rumour that she was engaged in the slave trade seems to be romantic nonsense, because slaving ceased in America 10 years before her launch.

95). "Lady of Avenel", named after a heroine in Walter Scott's novel.. Left, owners commissioned painting after re rigging as a Brigantine in 1877. (chapter 6).
96). Right Etching of her recovered figurehead, which was mounted above the entrance to a marine antique store in Poole until the 1980's. It is now privately owned in Germany. .

"David and Martha" Plymouth, 100 tons. Granite, Port Navas,1863.
Wrecked 1864, Braunton Sands. All lost.

"Delabole" Cutter rig. 1861, John and William Rendle plus one crew.
Wrecked 15. 09.1880.Cargo Granite. Clovelly lifeboat assisted, crew of three saved

"Guiding Star"
Brigantine 107 tons Built by Banks Jnr, KilpinPike in 1875. Registered London 1875J Wetherall, owner), Padstow 1898 (M.Thomas, owner), Plymouth 1924. George Turner (owner). 1875 Employed Newfoundland trade. Captain Tom Collings of Port Navas was skipper during the first world war when she was an armed merchant vessel. She laid up stern to below the Lime Kiln. Lost 1926

97). "Guiding Star" Left, commissioned owners painting 1875. 98). Right, alongside at Padstow, ?date

"Howard" (ex "Howard of Milford").
Official number 82977 . Flag code JGWL. Ports of registry 1884, Milford haven, 1901, Bideford, 1910 Scilly (George Phillips, owner). Built Neyland, W Wales by Joshua Mills, who owned 64/64 shares. 50 grt increased to 55 in 1885. Length 63.5 ft., beam 17.5 ft. draft 8.3 ft., Freeboard midships 9 ft. Decks 1, Rig Ketch. Elliptic stern, wood framed. Figurehead a dog's head. (perhaps she was named after Joshua Mills pet?).

Bought by Melchizadek Tremayne of Inow farm (32/64), W.M.Wilmot (16/64) and John Bevan, Tin Smelter of Redruth (16/64) on 10.5.1884 Mr Tremayne was Charles Rendles father in law, and she was the Rendle family ship. With Charles Rendle as skipper, Albert as mate, she carried the last load of Constantine granite to the Tower Bridge project in 1895.

On passage Swansea to Scilly with coal on 10.7.1910, she pulled off her weather chain plates in heavy seas off Lands End, and foundered 3 1/2 miles South of the Wolf rock. Crew were saved by a Pilot boat **"C 75"** Of Cardiff, and landed at Newlyn.

99). Drawing of Ketch "Howard", by Albert Rendle (1869-1936) grandson of the principal owner, Melchizadek Tremayne, owner. Albert's son and heir was named after her.

113

"Flying Foam" *of Bridgewater*

112gt; 88ft length x 20ft breadth 100 tons. Built Jersey in 1879. Port Navas was one of her regular ports of call in the coal trade. She was never fitted with an engine, and must have been a monster to dock on the lower quay! Wrecked Conwy Bay 1936 (below).

100). Wreck of topsail schooner "Flying Foam". Caught on a lee shore whilst anchored in Conwy Bay, July 1936. Few of the coastal vessels avoided similar ends of career. Right wreckage still present in 2005

"Leurier"
Referred to in Sidney Bate's first hand account, no record has been found of this vessel.

"Pet"
Official number 41126, Port of registry Padstow, 11.1857. Built Pugwash, Nova Scotia, by Levi Barton. 1857. Ketch rigged, 45tons, increased to 59 tons c 1875. Master till 1871, Captain John Bate (born 1804), then Steven Bate (born 1856) in July 1879. Coastal trade. Lost 3 miles of Strumble Head 1911.

"Trebiskin"
Official number 22179. Signal NKLV. Port of registry Padstow. Built S.T Bennet, Padstow 1859. 59 tons, increased to 69 tons Schooner rig. Owners Thomas Martyn, Padstow1876. Masters John Bate (born 1843) 1869, William Bate (born 1849) 1874, 1877, Sydney Bate (born 1856) was mate. Lost Worm's Head, Glamorgan, 04.1918

"Sarah Davies"
85 tons, Schooner, 1860. Built by James at Morben, Aberystwyth, for Captain David Davies. Later owned by Thomas Davies. Shipped coal to Port Navas in 1890's, and was in Port Navas at the 1891 Census. All crew members shared this surname. Sank in a gale, Clyde, 1912. Crew saved.

"Result"
Official number: 99937 122 **GRT** LOA 102 ft Beam:21ft 8 in, draft 7 ft 6 in Iron Built, Carrigfergus 1893. Owned by the Welch family of Braunton.Q ship in 1917 She traded channel ports including Port navas and Gweek until 1967. Now preserved in the Ulster Folk Museum.

"Water Lily"

Official Number 45226, Signal VCLB. Built Ben Blamey, Falmouth 1863. 62.49 grt, Length 65.7ft, beam 19.2 ft., draft 9.10 ft. Schooner rig. Owners Ben Blamey 1863-67, Captain William Bunt 1871-86, Masters Nicholls 1867, J.Pitick 1871, W.Bunt 1871, Sydney bate, 1874. Trade coastal . Lost to enemy action 1917.

101). Water Lily in Cardiff. She was sunk by German action in 1917.

"Fanny Crossfield"

The first of twelve three masted schooners built for James Fisher, by Paul Rodgers in Carrigfergus, in 1880. All wood, grt 119, length 95.6 ft., breadth 22.1ft, draft 9.8 ft. No figurehead. Visited brazil in her early career, under Capt. John Iddon. Sold to Grounds of Runcorn 1921,then Irish owners in 1936, and was fitted with an engine. The photograph in chapter 6 alongside the upper quay would be just after Irish acquisition. She ran aground in 1937 in Strangford Lough 1937, and was written off and broken up.

102). Above under full sail,

103). Above, on the bar, Falmouth.

115

104). *"Ethel Jane" and "RGD" of Teignmouth alongside in St Ives. Both carried Granite from Port Navas in the 1890's*

105). *Schooner "RGD", (left) discharging at St Ives*

"Queen of the Chase"

Official no. 13049. Signal Code LFJV. Built James Mayn, Little Falmouth, 1852./58, 1862/6 98 tons. 66ft 8in beam 17ft, draft 10ft. One deck, two masted topsail schooner. Carvel. Decks One, masts two.   Owners Edwin Pope (Principal), James Mayn (builder), John Michelle, John Curragh. Till 1881, then P.A Jeffrey (Falmouth) with Capt. W Bunt (Port Navas). 1902, Sydney Bate Masters: Capt. Cutliffe. 1867-73, Capt. Sydney Bate 1880-81, Capt. Webster 1882-87, Capt. Sydney Bate 1887-1905. Traded Fruit from Canary and Spain, Fish from Newfoundland, and coastal from 1881 on.

This was Sydney Bate's ship, as in the text Chapter 11. He was associated with her for 25 years, and when lost off Cardiff, his two sons were with him. All were saved.

106).. "Queen of the Chase" aground at Runcorn, date unknown.

107). Figurehead from "Queen of the Chase", salvaged after she was lost on Cardiff Sands. It represents a young Queen Victoria. Sold in 2013 at auction by Bosley's Military Auctioneers.

"Rob Roy"

Official Number 86123. Built Kitto, Porthleven, 1882 18 tons, LOA 43 ft., Beam 13ft 6Ins, Draft 6ft Straight stem, square stern. Two masts, ketch rigged. Wet hold midships for carrying oysters.
Owners John Tyacke 1882, Elizabeth Tyacke, widow, 1906.

Trade Local. Mainly Helford to Plymouth with spat or grown Oysters and fish.. Also carried coal, grain and timber.
Berthed at Merthen Quay, Mooring, 50 yds. up River from Merthen Hole.
Sold 1906, renamed **"Ailsa",** fitted with engine 1916. Lost 1925

"Sunbeam 2"

Built in 1929 by Denny of Dumbarton to George Watson's design, 636 tons, 195 ft. overall. This was the private yacht of Sir Walter Runciman MP, son of the Shipping magnate. She replaced a first **"Sunbeam"** (1874, built for Lord Brassey M.P, son of the railway engineer Thomas Brassey) and bought by Sir Walter in 1922).
Based on her predecessor, Sunbeam 2 was She was fitted with the wheel and figurehead reclaimed from the orignal "**Sunbeam**".   She was based in the Helford River 1939 to 1943 as **HMS Sunbeam** ,mother and accommodation ship for the Inshore Patrol Flotilla. She remains in commission, under the name **"Eugine Eugenides"** based in Piraeus, owned by the Greek Government. Currently under restoration.
Walter Runciman's 2nd son Sir Steven was a patient of Douglas Shepperd

108). Above left under sail 1930's

109). Above, the original Sunbeam of 1874,in which Lord and Lady Brassey circumnavigated the world. Runciman owned her before "Sunbeam2"

110). "Eugene Euginides", ex "Flying Clipper", ex "Sunbeam 2" is today, berthed in Piraeus. She appears to retain the figurehead, which was recycled from Lord Brassey's "Sunbeam" of 1874.
111). Above. The original ship was named after the 4 year old Brassey daughter, who died of scarlet fever the year before the ship was launched. The figurehead is her image.

"V.B. Lamb" ex "Catrina"

1882, London, 138 tons GRT, L.O.A. 116ft, beam 20ft. Triple expansion Steam, coal fired 28hp, twin screw. Steam winch with grab. Hold 6ft 6ins
Sand barge, built for Vectis Transport Co, Portsmouth, Dredging in the Solent.
Owners: Owen R Guard. Requisitioned for Barrage Balloon Service in the Thames Estuary During WW2.
Bought by Martin Vinnicombe at scrap value in 1955, and employed in Marine Salvage, on the wreck of SS Volnay. As such, she was the last commercial vessel using the port. The Vinnicombe's previously used a scrap steam drifter (nobody can recall the name), which was too deep to use the quay.
In 1958, now 76 years old, the ship developed a major leak in her (very thin) bottom plating. With the pumps on maximum, she was beached alongside the lower quay, where she settled. She was dismantled in situ, which triggered further indignation from the gentle folk of the village. In the court case that followed, the Vinnicombes were ordered to cease their operation, and awarded £15,000 compensation. An additional order prohibited the Lower Quay from future commercial use.

112). "V.B. Lamb" moored off Treath, 1957

113). "V.B. Lamb" alongside the lower quay, 1958, with "Freelance" in the foreground centre, and "Otter" on the oyster beach. Her final resting place was on the South wall of the quay

"Ryelands"

149 tons, built 1887, Nicholson & Marsh, Glasson Dock. Signal KJRG. Nearly lost by fire during building. Copper fastened. Traded mainly Liverpool, Guernsey, London, and China clay from Charleston. Bought by Walt Disney in 1947, and converted to replica a "**Hispaniola**" for the film Treasure Island.
Owned by Martin Vinnicombe 1957-59, and moored alongside the lower quay.

Later as "**Pequod**" in Moby Dick.
Lost by fire in 1970.

114). Three masted schooner "Ryelands"

115). Alongside the lower quay in 1959, disguised as "Hispaniola", & surrounded by BoT condemned ships lifeboats

116). As an exhibit in Scarborough, dressed as the "Pequod"

"Queen of the Fal 2"

71 tons, LOA 81 ft. Built by Cox and Co, Falmouth 1912. Single screw, triple expansion coal fired steam. Owned and operated by the River Fal SS Company, Requisitioned by the war office in 1942 for anti aircraft duty on the Clyde. Lost by mine.

117). SS "Queen of the Fal" under way in Carrick Roads Note trading schooners anchored off St Just

"Sunbeam"

Official number 145991. Tonnage: 10 gross 7 net Length 33.8 x beam 11.6. Depth in hold 5.4 ft. Built Looe 1913. Registered Plymouth. Owner in 1929 Alan Guilstone, Salcombe. 7hp engine added 1921. A sailing barge, engaged between the wars in transporting grain from Falmouth ships to local mills at Gweek. She was laid up and abandoned below Dinyan in 1938, and has been decomposing there ever since. A Petter petrol paraffin donkey engine was reclaimed by Ronnie Rashleigh. The keel is still visible opposite the higher quay. The mast was deployed for a number of years as the greasy pole in the regatta, until the competition was stopped on health and safety grounds—mainly because of splinters!

Appendix B: 19th century Granite Industry

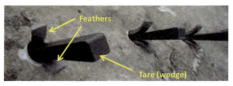

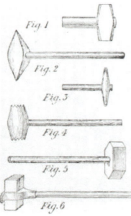

118). Above: Long and short feathers and tares /plugs

119). Far Left: Swell jumper in use and feather installation. One strike and turn.

120). Left: the range of hammers. Each had a specific purpose. Indirectly fuelled by Cornish Pasty! These were tough men!

121). Left. Bosahan quarry, owned by Freeman's. Beta Traction engine operating a scotch derrick, loading kerbing onto a 4 wheeled waggon . Freeman's had a fleet of five Fowler engines. Originally for road use, they were named after Greek alphabet, alpha, beta, gamma, epsilon, but the fifth was named Sophie, or "Her majesty". Some were adapted for powering crane s in the quarry. One suffered braking failure on Penryn hill, with drama but no fatality.

122). left: Alpha engine working a derrick in the same quarry. Ronnie Rashleigh's father operated the Alpha machine. These machines sustained demand for coal.

Hauling Granite

Below 123). left: About 1805. 3 of 4 horses are breaks.   124).Right: Similar size block, America 1920's

125). Above: 12 horses, pulling an 8 wheeled waggon, leaving Long Down.
126). Below: The load is approximately 524 cubic feet, weighing around 40 tons. A braking shoe is fitted to each of the 8 waggon tyres (2 waggons coupled). This consignment is believed to have been for the Wellington Monument, Stratfield Haye Hampshire. It went by train from Penryn..

A working day at Freeman's wharf, Port Navas

127). Above: Brunner & Lay Travelling Gantry of the type used in the upper quay— one rail was mounted on the (still surviving) wall, and the other on an iron frame 38ft away (now demolished)

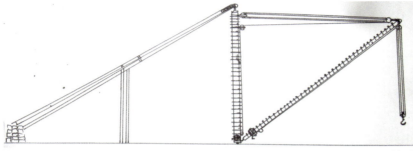

128). Above: Upper quay Scotch derrick, to estimated scale: Stabilising A frame spars 50ft, A frame posts 20ft, Samson post 32ft, Jib 45 ft. Manually operated winches at base for tackles. (jib height and lift hook). Samson Post swivels through a radius of 270 degrees.(see 46.). Granite purchase block on quay ("menhir" in 47, 48, 49). There was a similar apparatus on the lower quay. No image survives.

129). Left: Rough dressing shed of the type constructed on the upper quay (now replaced by the house)

130). Right: Scalping iron for dressing blocks

131). Freeman's yard Penryn, 1900. Larger and with more elaborate machinery than that at Port Navas Quay, and continued in operation until the early 1970's.

Appendix C Maps

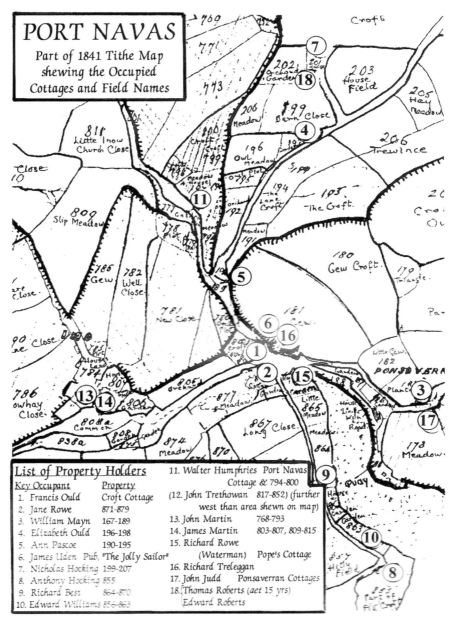

132). Tracing of 1842 Tithe map with Apportionments

133). Above: From sheet 6 of Martyns 1" to the mile survey of Cornwall, published 1748. The survey seems accurate, but Polperro and Chielow Creeks fell out of fashion.

134). C & J Greenwood Map 1827. After the first Ordnance Map. Names (Port Navas) locally provided.

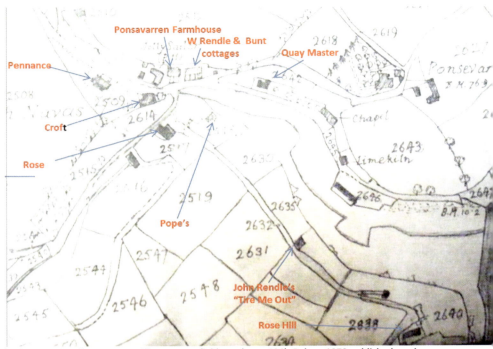

135). Above 1878 ordnance map, village centre *field numbers*, 136). Below. 1878 published version.

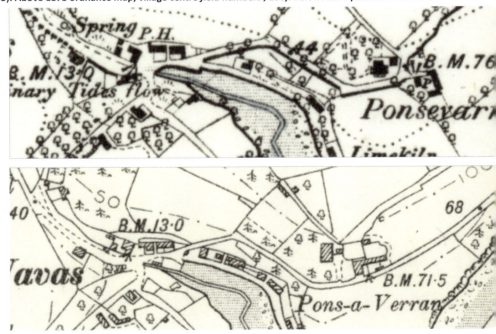

137)) Above. 1906 edition, showing recovered ground at creek head, manure store, Shearwater, Firleigh and the coal store. Pope's cottage still there, but no pub! Note the enlarged Ponsaverran and re routed top road.

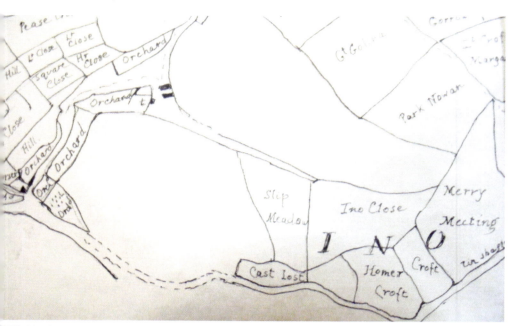

138). Merthen Estate map 1805. No Croft Cottage, and the mine at Merry Meeting field is marked as a Tin shaft (right). Merry meeting is named in the 1771 Merthen Estate Map, but no mine is recorded.

139). Above 1877 drawing and 140). Below 1878 published version of 6" Ordnance map showing Brogden's (Ex) mine. The spoil heap opposite Treviades Lane is still prominent today. Note 3 shafts, Treviades Lane top left

141). Above, Polwheveral: 1878, 142) Below, 1906

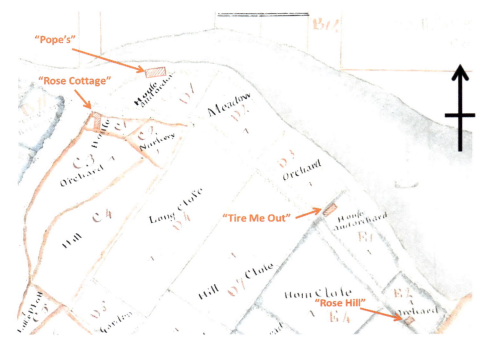

143). From Merthen estate map, 1771. Stylised representation of the creek, in which the cartographer has omitted the Chielo limb. Enlargement of creek below, shows meadows and orchards on creek side, with four cottages—Rose Cottage (previous structure), "Pope's" (now demolished), Tire me Out (redeveloped) and Rose Hill. All of these sites have been subject to rebuilds. Opposite bank (where quays were built) is virgin ground.

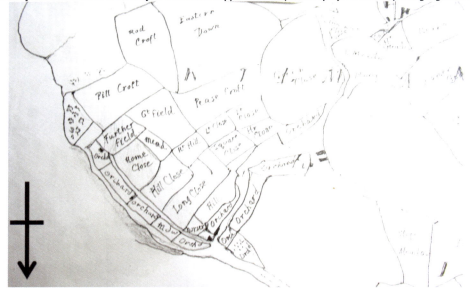

144). Tracing of Merthen estate map 1805 (Inverted from the 1771 above). Pope's has shrunk!

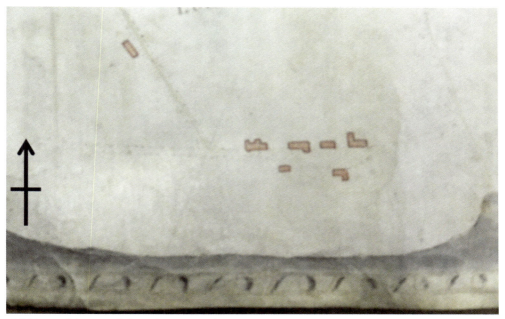

145). Lower Calamansack from the 1771 Merthen estate map. 7 cottages

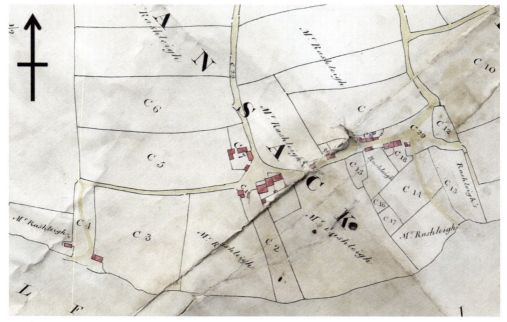

146). Merthen Estate Map, 1852. Lower Calamansack, when James Mayn has the lease. About 14 dwellings accommodating 50 people in the 1841 census.

Index

Adventurers	50	"Ethel Jane"	95, 15
Alet	29	Calamansack	22
Anna Maria Pender	31, 51	.... Higher	29
...............Mine	51	.............Lower	29, 65,
Arundel	30	Callevan	43
Austin 12/4	11	Camborne School of Mines	50
Austin, Sir William	63, 75	"Campion"	102
Ard	23	Carvedras quarry	43
Bannister, Eric	96,98	Carmenellis	35
Barrow	32	Celts	22
Barry Docks	48	Chatham Docks	49
Barton	27,28	Cheilow	31
Bate, Captain Sidney	90, 91-	Chestnut Cottage	70
.........Captain Steven	70, 90	Clodgy Lane	31
.........Euphemia	70	Coates, John	39
Bawden, Benjamin	32	Collings, Captain Tom	70
Beale, Fiona	106	...............Zoe (Exelby)	70
Belerion	50	Colwill, Philip	68
Bird, Geoff	106	.............Annie (Ould	68
Black Death	28	.............Edith	68
Blamey. M.L.	69	Cornish Oak	12
...............Thomas	69	Cornish Acre	
Blow house	31	Cornubian Batholith	42
Bonaemia Oetreaea	59	Cottage, the	65
Boaden, John	27, 87	Cove	30
Bruton, David	102	Coverack	20
.... Dollar	88	Croft cottage	44, 63, 69
Bunt, Captain William	66, 68	Cross, Tom	106
Burk, David	106	............Pat	106
Busk, Captain	75	Culch	53
Job's Water quarry	43	Danby, Edward	103
Borease quarry	43	"David and Martha"	112
Borlase	45	"Delabole"	65, 112
Bosahan quarry	43	Denton, Captain	75
Bosaneth		Devonium	15
Brill	43	Exelby, Elizabeth	68
Brogden Mine	48, 50, 51, 62, 67	Exeter, Diocese of	57
Bronze age	32	..................Bishop of	57
Bryanite	86	"Fanny Crossfield"	95, 113
Budock Vean	30	Firleigh	63, 74
Busk, Captain	75	Feathers	44
Calamansack	29	Flint axes	20
Diodorus Siculus	50	"Flying Foam"	113
Doyle, John	95,	Fortescue	30
"Duchess"	95	Fulling	31
"Duchy"	56	"Freelance"	98, 119
Duke of Cornwall	58, 75	Freeman's	67
Dumnonii	22	Freeman, John	44
Durant	30	Gabbroic clay	10
Eddystone Light	49	Gardiner, Dylis	!04
Egloshayle	30		

................Gwen	104
................Michael	104
.... Robert	104
................Stuart	104
Gealer, Mr and Mrs	75, 102
Gough	74
"Glider"	57
Goongillings	42
Goonhilly Down	21
Gough, Mr and Mrs	74
Granite	42-49 , 62
..........Carmenellis	42
Green, John	103
..............Margaret	103
Guano	69
"Guiding Star"	95, 113
Gunton, William	103
Gunton and Edwards	104
Hammerton,C.T.	63
Hamley	30
Handley, David	102
Harrison, Dorrie	107
................Hilda	107
Hawkins, Mary	104
Head	16
"Helford"	57
Heppel, George	103
High Cross	
Hacking, Sarah	65
Harris, John	08
"Hispaniola"	120
Hodges, Leonard	
..............Sidney	
..............Sidney	
............Willliam	57
Honey, Frank	39
Hosken, Richard	38, 44
.............., Emily Jane	38
..............William	44, 49
"Howard"	94, 113
Iccombe Wartha,	28
...............Wollas	28
Ice age	20
Inow	28
...........House	103
Iquique	67
"Iris"	95
Iron age	21-29
Job's Water quarry	43
Jolly Sailor	37,38
Jumper	44
Kerslake, David	107

Kestell, Walter	30, 35
Kiddlywinks	36
Keyham Steam Dock	22, 49
Knaar	110
Knibb, Irene	107
...........Leonard	107
"Lady of Avenel"	95
Laity, William	88
"Lamb V.B."	95, 119
Lane's Guide	48
Lestraynes quarry	43
Lizard	9
London Bridge	49
Lucas, Annabelle	74
...........James	74
Macfiheries	57, 74
Macdonald, Bruce	106
...................Caroline	106
.....................Roger	105
Magor	27
Maen Broathe	34, 57
Maen Pern	42, 43
Maen Pol	34, 42, 43
Maen Tol	42, 45
"Mary Jane"	102
Mangeons	103
Mayn,	34-39
...........Cottage	36
...........James (1727)	35
...........John, 1695	34
...........Jonathan 1782	35
Mayne, Ambrose	39, 63, 68
The Rev James	29, 67
...........James 1706	34
...........Josiah	38
.... Dr William Boxer	34, 54
...........William 1797	38
.... Mean, Symon	34
Meadows, Jeff	106
...................Tiff	106
Medieval	26-30
................ship	110
Merthen	22,32, 54
Merry Meeting	50
Mesolithic	20
Methodist Church	86
"Millie"	95
Mining	51-53
Moyle, John	70
...........John Arthur (Toby)	70
...........Elizabeth	70
...........Ellen	70
...........Harriet (Symonds)	

133

Mud	106,107
Mylor Slate	14
Myers, Jane	102
............Rodney	102
............Sally Ann	102
............Sue	102
............Tony	102
Nancenoy	31,34
Nelson's Column	49
Neolithic	15
.... vessels	110
Nicholas	27
Nottingham, Lucie	28
Ohlenslagger	98
Original Helford Oysterage	57
"Otter"	102
Ould, John	69
Oysters	53 - 59
Ostrea edulis	53
Painted ladies	8, 9, 98
Pascoe, Peter	63, 74, 75
Pennance	29,63, 70
Penrevren	26
Penryn	23
"Pet"	95
Plumtree Cottage	48
Plymouth	44
Pope's Cottage	64
Pope, Edwin	64, 94
Ponjerevah	53
Ponsavarren	30, 62
Polwheverel	28
Porthleven	55
Porthoustock	20
Portscatho	37
.... Slate	15
Port Navas Regatta	107
Prince Charles	58, 96
Protection of Ancient Monuments	48
Quay Masters House	70
"Queen of the Chase"	64, 92-94
"Queen of the Fal 2"	121
Rail, Farmer	70
Ramsgate Harbour	
Rashleigh, Ronnie	96
Ratcliffe, Joslynn	97
Rendle,Albert	65
............Arthur	88, 97
............Elizabeth Ann (Humphrey)	66, 70
..............EvaJ Jane	97
..............Gordon	97

.... Howard	58, 82, 84,
............John (1805)	65
............John (1833)	66, 90
..............Marjorie	97
..............Tim	98
..............William (1835)	66,90
.... Wiliam (1858)	90
Reskymer	32
"Result"	95
"Reliance"	57
Retallick	43
"R.G.D."	95, 115
Rickard, Harold	75
"Rob Roy"	55, 95, 117
Rogers, Graham.	65, 69, 96
..............Helena (Thomas)	9, 65
Roman	21-22
...........merchant vessels	110
Romansleigh	39
Roper, Brian	106
.................Dotty	106
Rose cottage	44, 63
Round	23-25
Round House	25
Rowe, William	87
Ruan Minor	35
"Ryelands"	120
Sailor Inn	
Scotch Derrick	48, 124
Scott, Charles	32, 52, 55
...........Caroline	52
Scott, Professor Peter	102
...........Margaret	106
Scribben, Liz	104 , 106
.................Patrick	104
Seager, John	39, 63
...........Revd Edward	39
Seaman's Chapel	64
Sessile oak	12
Seward, Dr	84
Shearwater	63, 67
Shepperd, Douglas,	
Silley, Jack	103
"Sir Francis Drake"	95
Smyth, Sir Warington Wilkinson	76
............Admiral William	76
Spargo, Brian	96, 98-102
...............Hugh	
..............Mildred (Rowlings)	102
Special Operations Executive	
St Keverne	10, 15
Stream	63

"Sunbeam" Sailing barge	9,121
"Sunbeam 2"	118
"Swallow"	95
Swell Jumper	44
Thomas,Fred "Skip"	74
...............Bunny	74
...............Robin	74
.............Sally	96, 106
.............Oliver,	96
Thomas, Richard	69
...............Elizabeth	69
...............Ellen	69
...............Minnie	69
Thomas, Captain	90
Thornpole	54
Tire Me Out	44, 66
Tolmen Stone	45
Tower Bridge	49
"Trebiskin"	91
Treculliacks quarry	43
Trefusis	28, 34,70
...............Baldwyn de	28
.............Peter de	28
.................Joan de	28
........................Richard	29
Treglidgewith quarry	43, 49
Trevean	68
Tremayne quarry	32
Tremayne, John	63
.................Mary Jane	66
.................Millie	97
Trevase quarry	43
Trewince	63, 75
Trewoon quarry	43
Trelivel	23
Trenarth	17, 26-28
.............Bridge	
Trenerth	26
Trengilly Wartha	32
Trerice	28, 107
Tresahor	43
Trevase	43
Trethowan, HS	112
Treviades	28
Trewardreva	32, 43
Trewince (Trewyns)	25-29
Trewoon	
Tyacke, John	55
Younger Dryas	20
Uden, Captain	74
Unilever	96

Variscan orogeny	
Vinnicombe	98
...............Martin	98
...............Rex	98
"Volnay"	98
Vyvyan	32,34
.................Sir Vyell	37
.................Sir Richard	51
Warington Smyth, Amabel	102
.... Barbara (Menzies)	102
...............................Herbert	76
.............................Nevil	76
.............................Bevil	76
.............................Nigel	76
.............................Pin	
.............................Rodney	76
....	
...................Elizabeth	76
Warren, John Stamford	65,
...............Henry	65, 97
...............Nelly	65
...............Tiny	65
...................Walter	65
"Water Lily"	91, 114
Waterloo Bridge	49
Water supply	63
Watt, Dee (Warington Smyth)	102
.........John	102
Webber, Thomas	39
.... Philip	39, 40
Wellington Monument	123
Wesley, John	86
Wheal	51
...........Bosaneth	51
...........Caroline	52
Westlake, Tom	
White, Farmer	75
Wilkins, Mike	98
Wilkins, Roger	107
...............Bernice	107
Williams, Edwin	70
Williams (Danby), Betty	96
..............., Giles	104
.................Nic	104
Williams, Stan	97, 103
Wings of Friendship	39
Winn, John Constantine	68
Winnianton	26
Winyard, Diana	103
Woodard, Sir Robert	102
.... Lady Rosalind	
Woolwich Steam Dock	49